PRAISE FOR
THE HOLY GHOST FROM A TO Z

"Liz Kazandzhy's *The Holy Ghost from A to Z* is a delightful and compelling read. I believe it will be very helpful to anyone who would like to increase the effectiveness of having the gift of the Holy Ghost in their lives."

—DAVID J. RIDGES
Best-selling author of *The Gospel Study Series*

"*The Holy Ghost from A to Z* puts a new light on our understanding of the Comforter. Organized in a fun, beautiful way, Kazandzhy packs the book with words of Church leaders and prophets of all ages. Any reader will come away feeling the love of our Heavenly Father and will feel instilled with a new relationship with the Holy Ghost. With lifetime lessons of peace and hope, this is a read for all to enjoy."

—SUSAN EASTON BLACK
Retired professor of Church history and doctrine
Brigham Young University

"Liz has done an amazing job of sharing some of the most insightful quotes and scriptures ever offered on the role of the Holy Ghost. The twenty-six topics discussed in this book each include a thought-provoking section to help you liken the function of the Holy Ghost to yourself, thus receiving more personal revelation. I highly recommend this book to anyone seeking to improve their life and feel the Spirit more strongly."

—RANDAL A. WRIGHT
Frequent Education Week speaker and author of
Achieving Your Life Mission

"I loved this book! Liz Kazandzhy has truly taught the most important of doctrines, clearly supporting them with the scriptures and words of prophets. Though the book is focused on the Holy Ghost, it also consistently directs readers to the Savior, and it illuminates God's character as loving and inviting rather than angry and vengeful. The chapters on forgiveness, peace, and having a humble heart are especially powerful. Overall, I was impressed with the thought that went into this book, and I look forward to using it as I teach my institute classes!"

—ANDREW HORTON
Institute instructor at Utah Valley University

"The Prophet Joseph Smith once said, 'No man can receive the Holy Ghost without receiving revelations. The Holy Ghost is a revelator.' In this first volume of the *A to Z* series, Liz Kazandzhy offers twenty-six things the Spirit has revealed to her. Utilizing a blend of scripture, modern prophetic utterance, and life-application, Liz walks her readers through some of the most important and empowering aspects of the Holy Ghost—discussing, illuminating, and applying the doctrine of the Spirit to the lives of her readers. This thoughtful book is sure to provoke introspection and encourage spiritual enhancement in the lives of receptive readers."

—ALONZO L. GASKILL
Professor of world religions
Brigham Young University

"Most of us are aware of the importance of the companionship of the Holy Ghost in our lives, but daily life often causes us to lose sight of how to do it. *The Holy Ghost from A to Z* is a practical guide that inspires not only encouragement and help but also enthusiasm to our efforts to live by the Spirit. This is a book I will return to many times in my own quest to do better."

—SHERRIE MILLS JOHNSON
Former professor of ancient scripture
Brigham Young University

"I was pleasantly surprised upon reading Liz's book about the Holy Ghost. Her use of scriptures and quotes by apostles and prophets gave her messages power and an edifying spirit. Her unique outline made it easy to read and understand true doctrine about this third member of the Godhead."

—JACK R. CHRISTIANSON, PHD
Best-selling author

"I can't begin to express how much I enjoyed this book. I've been a member of the Church my whole life, but I learned so much reading this. Each section is short and concise yet rich with doctrine about the blessings of receiving the gift of the Holy Ghost. Prepare to have your testimony of the Holy Ghost strengthened and your desires to follow Him increased!"

—AMY KLAUS

The Holy Ghost from A to Z

WHAT THE SPIRIT CAN DO FOR YOU

The Holy Ghost from A to Z

WHAT THE SPIRIT CAN DO FOR YOU

Liz Kazandzhy

CFI
An imprint of Cedar Fort, Inc.
Springville, Utah

ISBN 13: 978-1-4621-4274-3

Published by CFI, an imprint of Cedar Fort, Inc.
2373 W. 700 S., Springville, UT 84663
Distributed by Cedar Fort, Inc., www.cedarfort.com

Library of Congress Control Number: 2022935664

Cover design by Shawnda T. Craig and Courtney Proby

Printed in the United States of America

10 9 8 7 6 5 4 3 2 1

Printed on acid-free paper

To my parents, who taught me
to treasure the gospel of Jesus Christ.

Contents

Introduction

In February 1847, Brigham Young had a vision in which Joseph Smith appeared to him. As they talked, Brigham asked the Prophet if he had any counsel for the Saints. Joseph then "stepped toward him, looking [at him] very earnestly," and said the following:

> Tell [them] to be humble and faithful and be sure to keep the Spirit of the Lord, that it will lead them aright. Be careful and not turn away the still, small voice; it will teach them what to do and where to go; it will yield the fruits of the kingdom. Tell [them] to keep their hearts open to conviction, so that when the Holy Ghost comes to them, their hearts will be ready to receive it.[1]

Think about that for a moment. Out of all the counsel the Prophet Joseph could have given, his message focused on one thing—keeping the companionship of the Holy Ghost. And now, over 170 years later, President Russell M. Nelson has been emphasizing the same topic, declaring that "in coming days, it will not be possible to survive spiritually without the guiding, directing, comforting, and constant influence of the Holy Ghost."[2]

In order to follow this counsel, the first step is to receive the gift of the Holy Ghost as part of confirmation into The Church of Jesus Christ of Latter-day Saints. But simply having a gift *given* to you is not the same as receiving it, opening it, and enjoying its use.

---

1. Robert R. Worrell, "The Holy Ghost" (Brigham Young University–Idaho devotional, Mar. 18, 2003), byui.edu.
2. Russell M. Nelson, "Revelation for the Church, Revelation for Our Lives," *Ensign* or *Liahona*, May 2018, 96.

"For what doth it profit a man if a gift is bestowed upon him, and he receive not the gift?" (D&C 88:33) President Henry B. Eyring put it this way:

> We have the priceless promise of the Holy Ghost as a companion, and we also have true directions on how to claim that gift. These words are said by the Lord's authorized servant with his hands on our head: "Receive the Holy Ghost." At that moment you and I have the assurance He will be sent. But our obligation is to choose to open our hearts to receive the ministration of the Spirit over a lifetime.[3]

The purpose of this book, then, is simple—to "unwrap," so to speak, the gift of the Holy Ghost. In other words, my goal is to illustrate the many facets of the Holy Ghost—His roles, His capabilities, and the blessings He offers—so that you will be better able to recognize and receive Him into your life. I believe that if we truly understood how the Spirit could help us, we would be much more motivated to keep Him as our constant companion. And the more we learn about Him, the more we'll realize that "there is no greater blessing that can come into our lives than the gift of the Holy Ghost."[4]

How to Use This Book

This book is divided into 26 concise chapters corresponding to the letters of the alphabet. Each of these explores a certain aspect of how the Holy Ghost can help you.[5]

Because of this format, you don't necessarily need to read the book in order. In fact, the Spiritual Inventory Quiz (located directly after the Introduction) is designed to guide you to the sections that are most relevant to you right now. Based on your answers, you can

---

3. Henry B. Eyring, "His Spirit to Be with You," *Ensign* or *Liahona*, May 2018, 88.
4. *Teachings of Presidents of the Church: Gordon B. Hinckley* (2016), 119.
5. It should be noted that although this book covers many aspects of the Holy Ghost, it is in no way comprehensive.

start by reading those portions of the book that are most applicable and interesting to you.

However you choose to read this book—whether front to back or by skipping around—I'd encourage you to not rush through it. Take time to ponder what you read, answer the "Liken to Yourself" questions at the end of each chapter, and really consider how to apply what you learn. All these things will help you be "doers of the word, and not hearers only, deceiving your own selves" (James 1:22).

Lastly, I hope that you will gain as much from *reading* this book as I have gained from *writing* it. The Holy Ghost truly is incredible—an "ideal traveling companion," as Elder Larry R. Lawrence put it. This book has strengthened my testimony, deepened my understanding, and increased my desire to live worthy of the Spirit "so that when the Holy Ghost comes to [me], [my heart] will be ready to receive it." [6] I sincerely hope that it has a similar effect on you.

Spiritual Inventory Quiz

Read the following statements and put a checkmark by the ones you feel most apply to you. Then, refer to the chapter noted in parentheses after the statement.

If you'd rather not complete this activity, feel free to skip it and go directly to the first chapter.

- I want to experience greater joy and spiritual depth in my day-to-day life. (A)
- I feel like something is "off" in my life, even though I can't pinpoint why. (A)
- I want to get the very most out of my life. (A)

- I want to find greater satisfaction in my relationships. (B)
- I'm struggling with a relationship (for example, with a family

6. Robert R. Worrell, "The Holy Ghost" (Brigham Young University–Idaho devotional, Mar. 18, 2003), byui.edu.

member, ward member, coworker, friend, or someone else). (B)
- I'm feeling lonely and would like a friend, or I want to be better at making friends. (B)

- I've suffered a difficult loss. (C)
- I'd like help coping with the day-to-day challenges of life. (C)
- I'm feeling down and want to have my spirits lifted. (C)

- I need help making a decision or discerning between good and evil. (D)
- I'm not sure what the next step in my life should be. (D)
- I'm facing a problem that I don't know how to solve. (D)

- I know the right thing to do, but I'm hesitant to do it. (E)
- I feel discouraged about my weaknesses. (E)
- I'm not sure if living the gospel is worth it. (E)

- I want to know whether I've sufficiently repented of a sin. (F)
- I'm struggling to forgive myself for past sins. (F)
- I want to know my spiritual standing before the Lord. (F)

- I don't know what gifts and talents the Lord has given me. (G)
- I'd like help developing my gifts and talents or seeking new ones. (G)
- I want to better know how to use my gifts and talents. (G)

- I'm experiencing contention with another person. (H)
- I've run across a gospel doctrine, principle, or practice that I'm having a difficult time accepting. (H)
- I feel defensive after receiving correction from God or others. (H)

- I want to fill my life more with service to others. (I)
- I feel like I'm doing well spiritually but would like to become even better. (I)

- I'd like to strengthen my testimony of the Savior. (J)
- I want to experience the Atonement of Jesus Christ more personally. (J)
- I want to learn more about Jesus Christ's mission and ministry. (J)

- I'm struggling to understand a certain gospel topic. (K)
- I want to get more out of my gospel study. (K)
- I'd like to increase my intellectual abilities. (K)

- I'm doubting my self-worth and God's love for me. (L)
- I want to experience greater charity toward others. (L)

- I want to find people to share the gospel with. (M)
- I'm hesitant to share the gospel because I'm not sure what to say or do. (M)
- I fear rejection and opposition while doing missionary work. (M)

- I'm struggling to overcome a weakness. (N)
- I know I need to repent of a certain sin but am hesitant to forsake it. (N)
- I want to be better at recognizing and resisting temptation. (N)

- I feel overwhelmed by temporal concerns. (O)
- I'm having a hard time keeping an eternal perspective. (O)
- I want to see others and myself as God does. (O)

- I feel troubled about the problems happening in the world or in my personal life. (P)
- I'm experiencing feelings of fear and worry. (P)
- I'd like to find greater peace in my life. (P)

- I want to be healthier. (Q)
- I am dealing with pain, sickness, or other physical difficulties. (Q)
- I sometimes need a boost of physical or mental energy to accomplish a task. (Q)

- I want to be a more powerful gospel teacher. (R)
- I'd like to better remember the spiritual experiences I've had in the past. (R)
- I sometimes need to recall information (spiritual or non-spiritual) in a moment of need. (R)

- I want to improve my gospel study. (S)
- I have a hard time understanding the scriptures and how they apply to me. (S)

- I get bored studying the same gospel topics and scriptures over and over again. (S)

- I want to develop a deeper testimony of the gospel. (T)
- I want to better distinguish between truth and error—both in the world and within my own thinking patterns. (T)

- I want to better understand how the Spirit speaks to me personally. (U)
- I worry that I don't feel the Holy Ghost the same way others do. (U)

- I want to know how to determine whether a dream is from God or not. (V)
- I want to find more spiritual meaning in my dreams. (V)

- I want to keep myself physically safe. (W)
- I want to keep myself spiritually safe. (W)

- I'd like to know what God would have me change in my life. (X)
- I want to make changes in my life but I'm not sure where to start. (X)

- I want to better understand my purpose in life. (Y)
- I need help determining how to best spend my time and what endeavors to pursue. (Y)

- I feel I'm in a spiritual rut and want to get out. (Z)
- I want to increase my enthusiasm for gospel study and gospel living. (Z)
- I'd like my desires to be more righteous. (Z)

A

Brings **Abundance** to Your Life

"I am come that they might have life, and that they might have it more abundantly." (John 10:10)

This Will Help When . . .

- You want to experience greater joy and spiritual depth in your day-to-day life.
- You feel like something is "off" in your life, even if you can't pinpoint why.
- You want to get the very most out of your life.

Overview

What's the first thing that comes to mind when you hear the word *rich*? Often we think of someone abounding in wealth, having expensive possessions and more than enough money. But as alluring as this definition is, God has a much better type of richness in mind for His people: "a life filled with an abundance of success, goodness, and blessings."[7] It's a life of plenty, where you can satisfy your deepest longings by partaking of the Living Waters and the Bread of Life—sources of true joy that never run out.

President Spencer W. Kimball taught that "the abundant life . . . has little to do with the acquisition of material

7. Thomas S. Monson, "Living the Abundant Life," *Ensign*, Jan. 2012, 4.

things."[8] How then can you obtain it? The answer lies in the Holy Ghost, whose fruit is described in the scriptures as "love, joy, peace, longsuffering, gentleness, goodness, faith, meekness, [and] temperance" (Galatians 5:22). With an abundance of such qualities, it's no wonder Paul was able to say, "I have learned, in whatsoever state I am, therewith to be content" (Philippians 4:11). The Holy Ghost can likewise help you be content no matter your circumstances.

Take another look at the list of qualities the Spirit can foster: "love, joy, peace, longsuffering, gentleness, goodness, faith, meekness, [and] temperance." How much have you experienced these feelings lately? Now, what do you think your life could be like if those qualities were multiplied through the power of the Spirit?

On one end of the spectrum, you might feel like you're in a spiritual rut right now. Perhaps you're on spiritual "cruise control," going through the motions but without seeing much impact from them. Or you may feel like the spiritual aspects of your life equate to a quick "P.S." at the end of a letter that is otherwise full of temporal concerns. Something may just feel off to you, even if you can't determine exactly what.

If this is the case, perhaps it's time to seek out an added measure of the Spirit. Try following Elder Joseph B. Wirthlin's recipe for an abundant life:

- Love the Lord with all your heart, might, mind, and strength.
- Enlist in great and noble causes.
- Create of your homes sanctuaries of holiness and strength.
- Magnify your callings in the Church.
- Fill your minds with learning.
- Strengthen your testimonies.
- Reach out to others.
- Create of your life a masterpiece.[9]

---

8. Spencer W. Kimball, "The Abundant Life," *Ensign*, June 1979.
9. Joseph B. Wirthlin, "The Abundant Life," *Ensign* or *Liahona*, May 2006, 101.

Doing these things will bring a greater abundance of the Spirit, who can then bring an abundance of blessings into your life.

On the other end of the spectrum, maybe you've been feeling great spiritually! You're finding deep and helpful insights in your gospel study, enjoying a close relationship with God, and filling your life with the things that matter most.

In this case, you're clearly already experiencing an abundant life. But don't let that stop you from continuing to grow spiritually. The Lord taught, "For unto every one that hath shall be given" (Matthew 25:29). He will always have more to give you if you make yourself ready for it. If you continue to seek out God's will and strive to keep His commandments more and more fully, your "abundance [will be] multiplied unto [you] through the manifestations of the Spirit" (D&C 70:13).

No matter where you are on the spectrum of spirituality, remember that life will always be better with the Holy Ghost. If you try to find abundance without God's help, you will be like the ancient Israelites who "[forsook] . . . the fountain of living waters, and hewed them out cisterns, broken cisterns, that can hold no water" (Jeremiah 2:13). But if you instead seek His help, He will send you the Spirit, whose companionship is the "grand key to genuine success in this life, a key that opens the door to peace and happiness in this world and eternal glory in the world to come."[10] Truly, "The Holy Ghost can do for [you] physically, emotionally, mentally, and intellectually what no man-made remedy can begin to duplicate"[11]—so long as you keep Him abiding as your companion.

Liken to Yourself

- How would you describe "the abundant life"? What would that look like in your life?

---

10. Robert L. Millet, *The Holy Spirit: His Identity, Mission, and Ministry* (2019), 283.
11. Linda K. Burton, "Tuning Our Hearts to the Voice of the Spirit" (Church Educational System devotional for young adults, Mar. 2, 2014), broadcasts.ChurchofJesusChrist.org.

- Which fruit of the Spirit do you want more of right now: "love, joy, peace, longsuffering, gentleness, goodness, faith, meekness, [or] temperance"? Consider praying for this attribute and including it in your gospel study.
- Look back at Elder Wirthlin's list of advice. Which of those things stand out to you as something you should focus on right now? What can you do to implement it?

B

Strengthens Your **Bonds** with Others

"As we strive to build meaningful relationships . . . the Holy Ghost can guide us."[12]

This Will Help When . . .

- You want to find greater satisfaction in your relationships.
- You're struggling with a relationship (for example, with a family member, ward member, coworker, friend, or someone else).
- You're feeling lonely and would like a friend, or you want to be better at making friends.

Overview

Life's greatest joys—and greatest sorrows—come from our relationships with others. It's no surprise then that God wants to be involved in helping us strengthen our bonds with others, and He does so through His Spirit.

12. "Building Meaningful Relationships," *Ensign* or *Liahona*, Aug. 2018, 6.

For example, President Ezra Taft Benson taught, "The Holy Ghost causes our feelings to be more tender. We feel more charitable and compassionate with each other. We are more calm in our relationships. We have a greater capacity to love each other. People want to be around us because our very countenances radiate the influence of the Spirit." [13] Surely these characteristics of tenderness, charity, compassion, and love go a long way in strengthening relationships.

Not only can the Spirit help you become more loving, but He can also guide your efforts to improve your relationships. Have you ever wondered how best to minister to someone, how to grow closer to a family member, or how to resolve a conflict with a friend or coworker? These are all issues you can take to God through prayer, and He will answer you with revelation through the Holy Ghost. After all, God "knows all the thoughts and intents of the heart" (Alma 18:32). Therefore He knows how to best *reach* those hearts. If your desires are righteous, He can reveal to you the thoughts and needs of others so that you can make a positive difference in their lives.

In the case that *you* are the cause of a strained relationship, the principle is the same: "Through the guidance of the Spirit, [you] will be gently directed as to how to rebuild the relationships that may have been damaged through [your] choices. . . . As [you] seek to repair and rebuild relationships with the Lord and with [your] loved ones, [you] can begin to feel connected to others again."[14]

Now, what if your concern isn't about *improving* relationships but rather *obtaining* them? In other words, can the Spirit help you make friends? Surely we have all felt loneliness at one time or another, longing for a friend we can confide in and share meaningful memories with. And indeed, the Spirit *can* help. President Ezra Taft Benson taught that God will "raise up friends" for those "who

---

13. Ezra Taft Benson, "Seek the Spirit of the Lord," *Ensign*, Apr. 1988.
14. "Principle 3: Connect and Build Relationships," *Help for Pornography Users* (2019).

turn their lives over to God."[15] He can lead you to people who will lift your spirits, just as He can lead those people to you.

Lastly, the Holy Ghost can give you inspiration about how to *make* friends and also how to *be* a good friend. For example, if you struggle with shyness, He can give you the courage to go beyond your social comfort zone. If you struggle with personal habits or quirks that may be deterring your social life, He can prompt you to make changes. As one sister shared, "The Holy Ghost helps me to see my own weaknesses and how I can work to change my actions to help build [my relationships]."[16]

Heavenly Father loves you, and He cares about your relationships. As you seek and live worthy of His Spirit, He can help you continually strengthen your bonds with others.

Liken to Yourself

- How have you noticed the Spirit bless your relationships in the past?
- Think of a relationship you would like to improve. Pray for the Lord's guidance regarding that relationship, record the promptings He sends for how to improve it, and then make a goal based on those promptings.
- What do you struggle with the most when it comes to relationships? Ask God in prayer to help you overcome your weaknesses in this area.

---

15. Ezra Taft Benson, "Jesus Christ—Gifts and Expectations," *Ensign*, Dec. 1988.
16. Michele Burton, "Strengthening Relationships," *Ensign*, Oct. 2002, 24.

C

Comforts You

"Because of meekness and lowliness of heart cometh the visitation of the Holy Ghost, which Comforter filleth with hope and perfect love." (Moroni 8:26)

This Will Help When . . .

- You've suffered a difficult loss.
- You'd like help coping with the day-to-day challenges of life.
- You're feeling down and want to have your spirits lifted.

Overview

Mortality has been inherently uncomfortable ever since the Fall of Adam and Eve. However, God has always had a way to bring comfort to His children: through the Holy Ghost. As Elder Gary E. Stevenson taught, "Unexpected events in all our lives cause sadness, pain, and disappointment. Yet, amid these trials, the Holy Ghost serves us in one of His important roles—as Comforter, which is actually one of His names."[17]

---

17. Gary E. Stevenson, "How Does the Holy Ghost Help You?," *Ensign* or *Liahona*, May 2017, 119.

Perhaps the greatest need for comfort arises when we suffer loss, especially the loss of a loved one. Elder Craig C. Christensen shared his experience of when his father suddenly passed away at a family gathering:

> This unexpected event could have been devastating, especially for his grandchildren, raising questions that are difficult to answer. However, as we gathered our children around us, as we prayed and read the words of Book of Mormon prophets about the purpose of life, the Holy Ghost comforted each of us personally. In ways that are difficult to describe with words, the answers we sought came clearly into our hearts. We felt a peace that day that truly surpassed our understanding, yet the witness from the Holy Ghost was certain, undeniable, and true.[18]

Truly, the Spirit is the perfect Comforter—because He knows perfectly how to comfort each of us. As Professor Robert L. Millet wrote, "Because the Comforter knows all things (see D&C 42:17; Moses 6:61), he knows what lies deep within us, the longings and hopes and desires, the needs that often go unexpressed and thus unmet."[19] Similarly, Alma 7:12 says that the Savior "[took] upon him [our] infirmities . . . that he may know . . . how to succor [us]." The original Latin meaning of the word *succor* is "to run to help" or "hasten to the aid of."[20] And how does the Lord run to our aid? By sending the Holy Ghost to comfort us in precisely the way we need comfort.

Suffering a devastating loss isn't the only time we stand in need of solace. Indeed, the Comforter stands ready to comfort you *whenever* you need it—for problems big or small. "As the soothing voice of a loving parent can quiet a crying child, the whisperings of the

---

18. Craig C. Christensen, "An Unspeakable Gift from God," *Ensign* or *Liahona*, Nov. 2012, 13.
19. Robert L. Millet, *The Holy Spirit: His Identity, Mission, and Ministry* (2019), 118.
20. "Succor," Online Etymology Dictionary, etymonline.com.

Spirit can calm our fears, hush the nagging worries of our life, and comfort us when we grieve."[21]

What a fitting metaphor this is, considering the many reasons a child might cry—a fallen block tower, a change of plans, or simply being left alone for a minute. These may seem trivial to adults, yet to the child, they're very real problems. Likewise, whatever you're struggling with—no matter how trivial it may seem—your loving Father in Heaven longs to send His Spirit to comfort you. Craig C. Christensen said, "During times of trouble or despair or simply when we need to know that God is near, the Holy Ghost can lift our spirits, give us hope, and teach us 'the peaceable things of the kingdom,' [D&C 36:2] helping us feel 'the peace of God, which passeth all understanding' [Philippians 4:7]."[22]

There's yet another way the Comforter is described in the scriptures. In Doctrine and Covenants 88:4, the Lord says, "This Comforter is the promise which I give unto you of eternal life, even the glory of the celestial kingdom." This is the comfort of knowing you will see your loved ones again after this life. It is the comfort of knowing that all of your righteous strivings will not be in vain. And it is the comfort of knowing that "whether in this life or the next, all will be made right"[23] through the Atonement of Jesus Christ.

Now *that* is a comfort—and a Comforter—worth seeking.

Liken to Yourself

- When have you felt the comforting influence of the Holy Ghost before? How did He comfort you?

---

21. Gospel Topics, "Holy Ghost," topics.ChurchofJesusChrist.org.
22. Craig C. Christensen, "An Unspeakable Gift from God," *Ensign* or *Liahona*, Nov. 2012, 13.
23. Neil L. Andersen, "What Thinks Christ of Me?," *Ensign* or *Liahona*, May 2012, 114.

- What are some things that have been getting you down lately? Consider bringing those things to the Lord in prayer and seeking comfort from Him.
- How does the doctrine of eternal life—and God's plan of salvation—bring you comfort?

D

Gives You **Direction**

"If ye will enter in by the way, and receive the Holy Ghost, it will show unto you all things what ye should do." (2 Nephi 32:5)

This Will Help When . . .

- You need help making a decision or discerning between good and evil.
- You're not sure what the next step in your life should be.
- You're facing a problem that you don't know how to solve.

Overview

The scriptures contain story after story of people wandering in the wilderness—the Jaredites, Moses and the Israelites, Lehi's family, and even the Pioneers in early Church history. And doesn't this life also seem like a wilderness all too often? There's uncertainty, confusion, and chaos all around, and sometimes we just don't know which direction to go. Thankfully, God has given us "the gift of the Holy Ghost . . . as a sure guide, as the voice of conscience, and as a moral compass."[24] Let's look at a few ways the Holy Ghost can give you direction.

24. James E. Faust, "The Gift of the Holy Ghost—A Sure Compass," *Ensign*, May 1989.

First, the Spirit can help you discern between good and evil. Every day, we're confronted with the temptations and tactics of Satan, and he tries so hard to blur the line between good and evil. Wouldn't it be nice if we could know for sure what's right and what's wrong?

That's exactly what the Holy Ghost is for: "The Spirit of Christ is given to every man, that he may know good from evil. . . . And the way to judge is as plain . . . as the daylight is from the dark night" (Moroni 7:15). Truly, the Spirit can make the choice between right and wrong crystal clear. As Elder L. Tom Perry taught, "We do not need man-made rating systems to determine what we should read, what we should watch, what we should listen to, or how we should conduct our lives. What we do need to do is live worthy of the continued companionship of the Holy Ghost and have the courage to follow the promptings that come into our lives."[25]

Second, the Spirit can give you direction about important life decisions. From a relatively young age, up through our elderly years, we face decisions that significantly impact our lives—choices about education, employment, missionary service, marriage, child-rearing, and so on. Surely the Lord doesn't expect you to make these major life decisions on your own! Just as the Liahona led Lehi's family "in the more fertile parts of the wilderness" (1 Nephi 16:16) all the way to the Promised Land, so too will the Holy Ghost lead you on a prosperous life path—all the way to the celestial kingdom.

Lastly, the Holy Ghost can direct you in your day-to-day righteous endeavors. Although it's true that "the Spirit of the Lord is not likely to give us revelations on matters that are trivial,"[26] there are plenty of issues we face that God would be glad to help with through His Spirit—like how to handle a situation at work, how to get through to your child, what step to take next in your calling, or how to improve your health. So next time you're faced with

---

25. L. Tom Perry, "'That Spirit Which Leadeth to Do Good'," *Ensign*, May 1997.
26. Dallin H. Oaks, "Revelation" (Brigham Young University devotional, Sept. 29, 1981), speeches.byu.edu.

a problem you can't seem to solve, try following the invitation to "counsel with the Lord in all thy doings," and trust in the promise that "he will direct thee for good" (Alma 37:37).

It's worth noting that if you don't feel clear direction from the Spirit, you should continue to move forward in faith to the best of your ability and knowledge. After all, "it is not meet that [God] should command in all things" (D&C 58:26). So, instead of expecting to be "compelled in all things" (D&C 58:26) by the Holy Ghost, use your agency to make the best decisions you can while also remaining receptive to the Spirit. And in the absence of direct revelation, "proceed with trust . . . [knowing that] God will not let you proceed too far without a warning impression if you have made the wrong decision."[27]

Ultimately, there is no better guide to have by your side than the Holy Ghost. He will act as your "spiritual GPS to tell you . . . where you are and where you are going."[28] He also knows what is "good, better, and best"[29] for you, and He will help you make the *best* choices for your life and for eternity. As you strive to keep Him near, truly "the Lord thy God shall lead thee by the hand" (D&C 112:10), "direct thy paths" (Proverbs 3:6), "guide thee continually" (Isaiah 58:11), and "give thee answer to thy prayers" (D&C 112:10).

Liken to Yourself

- How has the Spirit helped you choose between good and evil before? How has He directed you in making the best decisions for your life?
- What's one decision you're facing currently that you could seek revelation about through the Holy Ghost?

---

27. Richard G. Scott of the Quorum of the Twelve Apostles, "Using the Supernal Gift of Prayer," *Ensign,* May 2007, 10.
28. M. Russell Ballard, "That the Lost May Be Found," *Ensign* or *Liahona,* May 2012, 100.
29. Dallin H. Oaks, "Good, Better, Best," *Ensign* or *Liahona,* Nov. 2007, 107.

- What are the biggest problems in your life right now that you haven't been able to solve yet? Have you sought God's help with these things? If so, what has He directed you to do?

E

Encourages You

"Shall we not go on in so great a cause? Go forward and not backward. Courage, [Saints]; and on, on to the victory!" (D&C 128:22)

This Will Help When . . .

- You know the right thing to do, but you're hesitant to do it.
- You feel discouraged about your weaknesses.
- You're not sure if living the gospel is worth it.

Overview

Take a look at some of the words used in 2 Nephi 31:20: "Ye must *press forward* with a *steadfastness* in Christ . . . and *endure* to the end" (emphasis added). That doesn't sound like a description of a casual stroll, does it? As President Henry B. Eyring said, "If you are on the right path, it will always be uphill."[30] But even though the journey of faith can be difficult—even grueling sometimes—the Holy Ghost can encourage you the whole way through. As Brother Milton Camargo taught, "The still, small voice is reaffirming,

30. Henry B. Eyring, "Raise the Bar" (Brigham Young University–Idaho devotional, Jan. 25, 2005), byui.edu.

encouraging, and comforting—and many times that's just what we need for the day."[31]

For example, have you ever known the right thing to do but *really* didn't want to do it? Maybe it completely goes against what your "natural man" (or woman) wants to do (see Mosiah 3:19), and you're struggling with that internal battle. Or maybe the idea to "do what is right; let the consequence follow"[32] honestly scares you because of what that consequence may be.

In either case, God can help. First, the Spirit can actually increase your *desire* to follow God's will, and second, He can encourage you to *act* on that desire. Even if choosing the right yields difficult consequences—such as persecution, loneliness, or discomfort—the Spirit will fill your heart with confidence that you did the right thing, blessing you with "the peace of God, which passeth all understanding" (D&C 4:7).

You may also need extra encouragement when you're confronted with your weaknesses. It's so easy to get down on yourself when you're faced with your own failures, and instead of turning to God in repentance, you may find yourself paralyzed by shame. In situations like this, allow the Spirit to work on your heart, communicate God's everlasting love for you, and drive away your fear and shame. With the help of the Holy Ghost, you can truly learn to "cherish the gift of repentance."[33] You'll be able to "acknowledge and face your weaknesses, but [not] be immobilized by them."[34] And you'll be able to "[grow] from failure to failure without any loss of enthusiasm."[35]

Consider one last example of when you may need encouragement. Malachi 3 tells of a people who compared the apparent success of worldly people with the difficulties experienced by the

---

31. Milton Camargo, "Ask, Seek, and Knock," *Ensign* or *Liahona*, Nov. 2020, 107.
32. "Do What Is Right," *Hymns*, no. 237.
33. "Young Women Theme," ChurchofJesusChrist.org.
34. Jörg Klebingat, "Approaching the Throne of God with Confidence," *Ensign* or *Liahona*, Nov. 2014, 37.
35. Lynn G. Robbins, "Until Seventy Times Seven," *Ensign* or *Liahona*, May 2018, 23.

people of God. They concluded, "It is vain to serve God: and what profit is it that we have kept his ordinance, and that we have walked mournfully before the Lord of hosts?" After all, "the proud [are called] happy; yea, they that work wickedness are set up; yea, they that tempt God are even delivered" (Malachi 3:14-15).

If you have ever felt the same way—wondering if living the gospel is even worth it, especially when the wicked seem so happy—take heart from the Lord's response in the verses that follow. "[They] that feared the Lord, and that thought upon his name . . . shall be mine, saith the Lord of hosts, in that day when I make up my jewels; and I will spare them. . . . Then shall ye return, and discern between the righteous and the wicked, between him that serveth God and him that serveth him not" (Malachi 3:16-18; italics added).

The eternal rewards of righteousness—and the eternal consequences of sin—may not always be visible with mortal eyes, but the Spirit can help you see them with your spiritual eyes. And with that eternal perspective, you will truly be able to "press forward, feasting upon the word of Christ, and endure to the end . . . [until] thus saith the Father: Ye shall have eternal life" (D&C 31:20).

Liken to Yourself

- What difficult things have you been able to do in your life because of the encouragement of the Holy Ghost?
- What are some of your weaknesses that tend to get you down? The next time you feel discouraged about your sins and weaknesses, what could you do to invite the Spirit into your life to help encourage you?

F

Conveys God's **Forgiveness**

"By the sanctifying power of the Holy Ghost as our constant companion, we can always retain a remission of our sins." (Elder David A. Bednar)[36]

This Will Help When . . .

- You want to know whether you've sufficiently repented of a sin.
- You're struggling to forgive yourself for past sins.
- You want to know your spiritual standing before the Lord.

Overview

Many of us understand that repentance is an inevitable part of our mortal and eternal progress. As Elder Lynn G. Robbins put it, "Repentance isn't [God's] backup plan in the event we might fail. Repentance *is* His plan, knowing that we will."[37] That being said,

36. David A. Bednar, "Always Retain a Remission of Your Sins," *Ensign* or *Liahona*, May 2016, 62.
37. Lynn G. Robbins, "Until Seventy Times Seven," *Ensign* or *Liahona*, May 2018, 22.

how do you know when the Lord has accepted your repentance? How can you know if you've been forgiven?

The answer is surprisingly simple, and it comes in the form of the Holy Ghost. Elder Tad R. Callister explained it this way:

> If you feel the Spirit—when you pray, read the scriptures, teach, testify, or at any other time—then that is your witness that you have been forgiven or, alternatively, that the cleansing process is taking place, for the Spirit cannot dwell in an unholy tabernacle [see Alma 7:21]. In most cases the cleansing process takes time because our change of heart takes time, but in the interim, we can proceed with the confidence that God approves of our progress as manifested by the presence of His Spirit.[38]

In other words, even though repentance is a process, you don't have to wait until the *end* of that process to feel God's love, approval, and even forgiveness. This is why Amulek taught that "if ye will repent and harden not your hearts, immediately shall the great plan of redemption be brought about unto you" (Alma 34:31). *Immediately*—not eventually. Or, in the words of Elder Jeffrey R. Holland, "It takes exactly as long to repent as it takes you to say 'I'll change'—and mean it."[39]

So, if you are wondering if you've sufficiently repented of your sins, and if the Lord truly forgives you, the answer really is simple: do you feel the Holy Ghost in your life?

If you can feel the Spirit, you can know for a surety that you are on the right track, that God approves of your progress, and that you can move forward with your life—*and* forgive yourself. On the other hand, if you find yourself lacking the Spirit, that's a pretty clear sign that you need to repent. However, don't let that fact discourage you.

---

38. Tad R. Callister, "How Do I Know When I Am Forgiven?," *New Era*, Aug. 2012, 26.
39. Jeffrey R. Holland, "For Times of Trouble" (Brigham Young University devotional, Mar. 18, 1980), speeches.byu.edu.

Elder Richard G. Scott said, "Remember, repentance is not punishment. It is the hope-filled path to a more glorious future."[40]

The Lord is not waiting to censure you for your sins—He is waiting to embrace you for your righteous efforts. And if you fear His disappointment in you, try to remember instead "how great is his joy in the soul that repenteth!" (D&C 18:10) As Linda S. Reeves said, "Perhaps at no other time do we feel the divine love of the Savior as abundantly as we do when we repent,"[41] and the Holy Ghost will convey that glorious love to you—from the very moment you begin to repent.

Liken to Yourself

- Do you have a hard time forgiving yourself? Why do you think this is? What can you learn from God's example of forgiveness that can help you forgive yourself?
- Is there anything the Spirit is prompting you to repent of? What can you do to change this thing? What blessings do you think await you when you do?

---

40. Richard G. Scott, "Personal Strength through the Atonement of Jesus Christ," *Ensign* or *Liahona*, Nov. 2013, 84.
41. Linda S. Reeves, "Claim the Blessings of Your Covenants," *Ensign* or *Liahona*, Nov. 2013, 118.

G

Expands Your **Gifts** and Talents

"Deny not the gifts of God, for they are many; and they come from the same God. . . . They are given by the manifestations of the Spirit of God unto men, to profit them." (Moroni 7:8)

This Will Help When . . .

- You don't know what gifts and talents the Lord has given you.
- You'd like help developing your gifts and talents or seeking new ones.
- You want to better know how to use your gifts and talents.

Overview

Elder Henry D. Taylor taught that "God has granted to each of us gifts, talents, and abilities, with the hope and expectation that we will increase and use them—not for selfish purposes, but for the benefit of others."[42] These include the gifts of the Spirit (see Moroni 7:8-18; D&C 46:8-26), natural talents, and inherent qualities that bless the lives of others. And when it comes to recognizing,

42. Henry D. Taylor, "Gifts and Talents," *New Era*, Aug. 1977.

developing, and using your gifts and talents, the Holy Ghost will be your ultimate helper.

As we know from John 16:13, "The Spirit . . . will guide you into all truth." This includes the truth about your own gifts and talents. You may clearly recognize some of your gifts, but others may not be so apparent until you seek revelation through the Spirit. To help you with this, write a list of your gifts and talents, and when you run out of ideas, pray for the Spirit to make known to you any you may have missed. Continue to jot down ideas as they come to you, immediately after your prayer as well as in the days (and even weeks) to come. You may be surprised at how many gifts the Lord has truly given you!

After you recognize your gifts and talents, the next step is to develop them. The Spirit can reveal to you how best to cultivate your talents, lead you to opportunities for further development, and encourage you to keep improving. And while it's true that some people develop their talents without such direct intervention from God, that shouldn't deter you from involving God in the process. As President Ezra Taft Benson taught, "Men and women who turn their lives over to God will find out that He can make a lot more out of their lives than they can."[43] The Spirit will accelerate your growth, expand your abilities, and increase your endurance as you seek to develop.

Finally, there is the task of actually *using* your gifts and talents for good. If you miss this step, you're akin to that "unprofitable servant . . . [who] was afraid, and went and hid [his] talent in the earth" (Matthew 25:25, 30). After all, these gifts are not meant to be ours alone—God specifically gives them "that all may be profited thereby" (D&C 46:12).

So, once you know your gifts and talents, actively look for ways to use them in service to others. This includes actively seeking *revelation* to know how best to use them. You obviously don't have to

43. Ezra Taft Benson, "Jesus Christ—Gifts and Expectations" (Brigham Young University devotional, Dec. 10, 1974), speeches.byu.edu.

wait for a prompting from the Spirit to make use of your gifts, but be very sensitive to the promptings that *do* come. In other words, be "anxiously engaged" (D&C 58:27) in good causes while also "[letting] the Holy Spirit guide."[44]

Lastly, don't ever feel limited to a select few gifts and talents that you call your own. God has encouraged us to "seek . . . earnestly the best gifts, always remembering for what they are given" (D&C 46:8). Whatever gift you feel inspired to seek, counsel with the Lord to know how to obtain it, for "he that asketh in Spirit shall receive in Spirit" (D&C 46:28).

So, whether you need help recognizing, developing, or using your gifts and talents, the Holy Ghost is sure to be a valuable companion to you. And as your repertoire of gifts expands, always remember "that every good gift cometh of Christ" (Moroni 10:18) and that "ye must give thanks unto God in the Spirit for whatsoever blessing ye are blessed with" (D&C 46:32).

Liken to Yourself

- Follow the suggested activity to write a list of your gifts and talents, and ask the Spirit to reveal to you what you may have missed.
- What's one thing you can do in the next week to *develop* one of your talents, spiritual gifts, or divine attributes?
- What's one thing you can do in the next week to *use* your talents and spiritual gifts for the profit of others?
- Which spiritual gift would you like to *seek out*, and how could you do so?

44. "Let the Holy Spirit Guide," *Hymns*, no. 143.

H

Softens Your **Heart**

"I thank my great God that he has given us a portion of his Spirit to soften our hearts." (Alma 24:8)

This Will Help When . . .

- You're experiencing contention with another person.
- You've run across a gospel doctrine, principle, or practice that you're having a difficult time accepting.
- You feel defensive after receiving correction from God or others.

Overview

In the index to the triple combination, the entry for "hardheartedness" contains a list of related topics, such as "Contention; Doubt; Hate; Pride; Rebel; Resist; Stiffnecked; Stubbornness; Unbelief; Wicked." If you find yourself personally relating to any of those words, it's a sign you need to soften your heart. Thankfully, the Holy Ghost is very good at helping with this. As Professor Robert L. Millet wrote, "The visitation of the Spirit leads to a softening of the heart, a malleability, a tenderness, an openness to the ways of the Master."[45]

---

45. Robert L. Millet, *The Holy Spirit: His Identity, Mission, and Ministry* (2019), 218.

One area in which we often need to soften our hearts is in our relationships, particularly during times of contention. Elder Steven E. Snow taught the following:

> Unnecessary pride can dissolve family relationships, break up marriages, and destroy friendships. It is especially important to remember humility when you feel contention rising in your home. Think of all the heartache you can avoid by humbling yourself to say, "I'm sorry"; "That was inconsiderate of me"; "What would you like to do?"; "I just wasn't thinking"; or "I'm very proud of you." If these little phrases were humbly used, there would be less contention and more peace in our homes.[46]

When you're "in the wrong," the Spirit can help you to see that and move you toward making amends. And even when you're "in the right," the Spirit can *still* help you to soften your heart toward the other person, see things from their perspective, feel greater love for them, and extend to them forgiveness. Remember that "yielding to emotions such as anger or hurt or defensiveness will drive away the Holy Ghost,"[47] whereas yielding to the Holy Ghost will allow the Lord to "take away the stony heart out of your flesh" and give you "a new heart" and "a new spirit" (Ezekiel 36:26).

Another time it's important to seek out greater humility is when you come across gospel doctrines, principles, or practices that are confusing or even distressing to you. These topics can become a major stumbling block to your faith if you choose to harden your heart because of them. Instead, what you ought to do is actively strive to *soften* your heart—from the very moment you begin to feel doubts creeping in. Then you'll be able to continue to seek understanding with the protective influence of the Spirit. You will probably not find all the answers you seek—at least in this lifetime—but

---

46. Steven E. Snow, "Be Thou Humble," *Ensign* or *Liahona*, May 2016, 37.
47. Richard G. Scott, "How to Obtain Revelation and Inspiration for Your Personal Life," *Ensign* or *Liahona*, May 2012, 45.

the Holy Ghost can lead you to greater understanding and also help you "doubt your doubts before you doubt your faith."[48] And you, like Nephi, will be able to say, "I do not know the meaning of all things . . . [but] I know that [God] loveth his children" (1 Nephi 11:17).

Lastly, it's very easy to find yourself with a hard heart when confronted with correction—whether from God or from others. When someone points out something legitimately wrong with us, it can be very difficult to face, and we often react defensively. However, the Spirit can do two things to soften your heart in such circumstances. First, He can help you determine if the correction is valid and you really *should* change that thing, thus helping break down your pride. And second, He can affirm your worth and communicate to you God's love, thus keeping you from spiraling downward in shame.

If you seek the Spirit's companionship in times of correction, you can avoid both pride *and* shame, and you can focus on improving instead. As President Gordon B. Hinckley taught, "Growth comes of correction. Strength comes of repentance. Wise is the man who can acknowledge mistakes pointed out by others and change his course."[49] Always remember that "whom the Lord loveth he chasteneth" (Hebrews 12:6). And by responding to that chastening with a soft heart, you will come one step closer to achieving the eternal goal found in Matthew 5:48: "Be ye therefore perfect, even as your Father which is in heaven is perfect."

Liken to Yourself

- How can you tell when your own heart is figuratively "soft" or "hard"? In other words, how do you feel when you're being humble versus when you're being prideful?
- In what circumstances are you most likely to harden your heart? In moments like these, what could you do to invite the Spirit back into your life to soften your heart?

---

48. Dieter F. Uchtdorf, "Come, Join with Us," *Ensign* or *Liahona*, Nov. 2013, 23.
49. Gordon B. Hinckley, "The Continuing Pursuit of Truth," *Ensign*, Apr. 1986.

- What is your usual reaction to receiving correction? Do you gravitate more toward pride or shame? How do you think the Lord would have you respond, and why?

I

Inspires You to Do Good

"Put your trust in that Spirit which leadeth to do good—yea, to do justly, to walk humbly, to judge righteously." (D&C 11:12)

This Will Help When . . .

- You want to fill your life more with service to others.
- You feel like you're doing well spiritually but would like to become even better.

Overview

President Thomas S. Monson is well-known for his selfless service and desire to follow the Spirit. He said, "The sweetest experience I know in life is to feel a prompting and act upon it and later find out that it was the fulfillment of someone's prayer or someone's need. And I always want the Lord to know that if He needs an errand run, Tom Monson will run that errand for Him."[50] These promptings to do good come from the Holy Ghost, and such inspiration is available to all who strive to live righteously.

---

50. William R. Walker, "Follow the Prophet" (Church Educational System devotional for young adults, May 5, 2013), broadcasts.ChurchofJesusChrist.org.

Because the Lord "knoweth all things," and "all things are present before [His] eyes" (D&C 38:2), He knows exactly *who* needs help, what *kind* of help they need, and *when* they need it. And because "we are the Lord's hands here upon the earth,"[51] we have the unique blessing of providing that help by following the promptings of the Spirit.

The Holy Ghost can inspire you "to reach out to someone in need, family and friends in particular," and He can "point [you] to opportunities to teach the gospel, to bear testimony of the Restoration and Jesus Christ, to offer support and concern, and to rescue one of God's precious children."[52] As you follow this inspiration and fill your life with service to others, you will experience a greater sense of purpose, deeper spiritual growth, and more profound joy, because "we receive the Holy Spirit best when we are focused on serving others."[53] As President Dieter F. Uchtdorf taught, "As we lose ourselves in the service of others, we discover our own lives and our own happiness."[54]

Another way the Spirit can inspire you to do good is by prompting you to be better. Sometimes this means calling you to repentance by gently (but boldly) pointing out when you have sinned. But at other times, it means simply nudging you in ways that further your spiritual growth—encouraging you to "lengthen your stride,"[55] "stand a little taller, rise a little higher, [and] be a little better."[56]

Elder Bednar once described this process of repentance and spiritual growth in his talk "Clean Hands and a Pure Heart." He said the following:

---

51. Thomas S. Monson, "Serve the Lord with Love," *Ensign*, Feb. 2014.
52. Ronald A. Rasband, "Let the Holy Spirit Guide," *Ensign* or *Liahona*, May 2017, 96.
53. Henry B. Eyring, "Inspired Ministering," *Ensign* or *Liahona*, May 2018, 64.
54. Dieter F. Uchtdorf, "Happiness, Your Heritage," *Ensign* or *Liahona*, Nov. 2008, 119.
55. This phrase is attributed to President Spencer W. Kimball, who used it in his addresses on several occasions.
56. Gordon B. Hinckley, "The Quest for Excellence" (Brigham Young University devotional, Nov. 10, 1998), speeches.byu.edu.

> The gospel of Jesus Christ encompasses much more than avoiding, overcoming, and being cleansed from sin and the bad influences in our lives; it also essentially entails doing good, being good, and becoming better. Repenting of our sins and seeking forgiveness are spiritually necessary, and we must always do so. But remission of sin is not the only or even the ultimate purpose of the gospel. To have our hearts changed by the Holy Spirit such that "we have no more disposition to do evil, but to do good continually" [Mosiah 5:2], as did King Benjamin's people, is the covenant responsibility we have accepted.[57]

Whether you're looking for a remission of your sins or just the opportunity to improve even more, seek the inspiration of the Spirit. By following His promptings, you can experience both the "*cleansing and redeeming power* that helps us to overcome sin" and the "*sanctifying and strengthening* power that helps us to become better than we ever could by relying only upon our own strength"[58]—all of which is possible only because of the Atonement of Jesus Christ.

Liken to Yourself

- How does the Spirit usually speak to you? If He were to prompt you to reach out to someone else in service, what do you think that prompting would feel like to you?
- When you think of sins you need to repent of, what does the Spirit bring to mind? When you think of ways you can "lengthen your stride" and "stand a little taller," what does the Spirit bring to mind?

---

57. David A. Bednar, "Clean Hands and a Pure Heart," *Ensign* or *Liahona*, Nov. 2007, 81–82.
58. Ibid., 82.

J

Testifies of **Jesus Christ**

"It is only through the power of the Holy Ghost that we can receive a sure testimony of God the Father and His Son, Jesus Christ."[59]

This Will Help When . . .

- You'd like to strengthen your testimony of the Savior.
- You want to experience the Atonement of Jesus Christ more personally.
- You want to learn more about Jesus Christ's mission and ministry.

Overview

As this book clearly shows, the Holy Ghost can do so many things for us. However, it's important to remember that "the *principal* mission of the Holy Ghost is to testify of our Heavenly Father and His Beloved Son, Jesus Christ."[60] In fact, the Spirit is essential for you to gain a testimony of the Savior, for "no man can say that Jesus is the Lord, but by the Holy Ghost" (1 Corinthians 12:3).

---

59. "The Holy Ghost Testifies of Truth," *Ensign*, Mar. 2010, 10.
60. Joseph B. Wirthlin, quoted in *The Gospel and the Productive Life Student Manual (Religion 150)* (2017), 8; emphasis added.

During Christ's ministry, He asked the Pharisees a question that we all ought to ask ourselves: "What think ye of Christ?" (Matthew 22:42). Today, some people ridicule Him as a fraud, while others revere Him "as the greatest teacher who ever lived, but deny that he is Messiah, Savior, or Redeemer."[61] But the truth lies in the words of the apostle Peter: "Thou art the Christ, the Son of the living God" (Matthew 16:16). And how did Peter know that? As the Savior explained, "Flesh and blood hath not revealed it unto thee, but my Father which is in heaven" (Matthew 16:17).

You too can obtain a testimony of Jesus Christ's divinity by the power of the Holy Ghost. Elder Joseph B. Wirthlin taught that "the Holy Ghost will help you learn more about Heavenly Father and Jesus Christ. He will enlighten your mind as you ponder and study the scriptures each day."[62] As you study the gospel, the Spirit can expound to you Christ's teachings, reveal deeper meaning in His parables, give you insights about His character, and teach you how to become more like Him. John 17:3 teaches us that "this is life eternal, that [we] might know . . . the only true God, and Jesus Christ, whom [He] hast sent." And how will you know Them? Through "the Holy Ghost, which witnesses of the Father and the Son" (2 Nephi 31:18).

Knowing that Jesus Christ is the Savior of the world is a vital first step. But knowing that He is *your* Savior will make all the difference in your life. Consider how Christ interacted with the Nephites "one by one" (3 Nephi 11:15) after His Resurrection:

> "Come forth unto me" wasn't a general statement. He wanted them to go forth one b*y one*. . . . He wanted them to individually come to Him, to meet Him, and to receive an up close and personal witness that He really is the Savior of the world. He wanted them to feel the prints in His hands and

61. Dallin H. Oaks, "'What Think Ye of Christ?'," *Ensign*, Nov. 1988.
62. Joseph B. Wirthlin, quoted in *The Gospel and the Productive Life Student Manual (Religion 150)* (2017), 8.

> feet—the marks of the Atonement He'd completed just for them. . . .
>
> Jesus Christ still calls us to come unto Him, and that invitation is still extremely personal. He is the Savior of the world, but He is also the Savior of *you*. . . . Because of His atoning sacrifice, He can comfort and strengthen you personally. And He wants you to know that for yourself.[63]

As you seek a personal relationship with Jesus Christ, the Spirit will help you feel His love, experience the redeeming and healing power of His Atonement, and find comfort from the One who "[took] upon him [your] infirmities . . . that he may know . . . how to succor [you]" (Alma 7:12). And when you're asked in a temple recommend interview, "Do you have a testimony of the Atonement of Jesus Christ and of His role as your Savior and Redeemer?" you will be able to confidently—with reverence and deep gratitude—answer yes.

Liken to Yourself

- What is your testimony of Jesus Christ? How have you gained that testimony?
- What do you think is the difference between believing in Jesus Christ as *the* Savior and believing in Him as *your* Savior? Why do you think some people have a hard time accepting Him as their personal Savior?
- What's one thing you can do this week to seek a deeper testimony of Jesus Christ and a closer relationship with Him?

---

63. Charlotte Larcabal, "The Savior of You," *New Era*, Apr. 2018, 6.

K

Deepens Your **Knowledge**

"And from time to time, as shall be manifested by the Comforter, [you shall] receive revelations to unfold the mysteries of the kingdom." (D&C 90:14)

This Will Help When . . .

- You're struggling to understand a certain gospel topic.
- You want to get more out of your gospel study.
- You'd like to increase your intellectual abilities.

Overview

God has always encouraged His people to "seek learning, even by study and also by faith" (D&C 88:118). First and foremost, the Lord wants us to seek knowledge "in all things that pertain unto the kingdom of God" (D&C 88:78), and the Holy Ghost can help with this in a variety of ways.

For one, He can enlighten your understanding. The Lord said, "For by my Spirit will I enlighten them, and by my power will I make known unto them the secrets of my will" (D&C 76:10). For example, the Holy Ghost can help you comprehend difficult scriptural passages, leading you to find profound personal application in what you otherwise may have glossed over. Or He can help you make connections between gospel doctrines, giving you "aha!" moments that feel like a spiritual lightbulb turning on.

Such moments of spiritual insight can come to all of us, whether we're a recent convert or a lifelong Church member. Even the prophet, President Russell M. Nelson, declared, "I am a different man!"[64] after dedicating Himself to a deeper study of Jesus Christ. If the Holy Ghost can help a ninety-two-year-old prophet of God find deeper meaning in the scriptures, surely He can help us too!

Beyond just helping you gain a better *understanding* of gospel topics, the Spirit is the source of *testimony* as well. As President Dallin H. Oaks described, "A testimony of the gospel is a personal witness borne to our souls by the Holy Ghost that certain facts of eternal significance are true."[65] A knowledge of gospel topics is important, but it is ultimately your testimony that will lead to your true conversion and eternal progression. In the words of Elder David A. Bednar, "We should know the gospel is true and be true to the gospel."[66]

Lastly, the Holy Ghost isn't limited to just helping in spiritual matters. After all, God values education about a vast array of temporal subjects, including the following:

> Of things both in heaven and in the earth, and under the earth; things which have been, things which are, things which must shortly come to pass; things which are at home, things which are abroad; the wars and the perplexities of the nations, and the judgments which are on the land; and a knowledge also of countries and of kingdoms. (D&C 88:79)

By growing in knowledge, you can "be prepared in all things when [the Lord] shall send [you]" forth in service (see D&C 88:80). As President Russel M. Nelson taught, "Education is the difference

64. Neil L. Andersen, "We Talk of Christ," *Ensign* or *Liahona*, Nov. 2020, 89.
65. Dallin H. Oaks, "Testimony," *Ensign* or *Liahona*, May 2008, 26.
66. David A. Bednar, "Converted unto the Lord," *Ensign* or *Liahona*, Nov. 2012, 109.

between *wishing* you could help other people and *being able* to help them."[67]

Because of this, never hesitate to involve the Holy Ghost in deepening your knowledge of temporal matters, for "all things unto [God] are spiritual" (D&C 29:34). Whether you're pursuing a formal education, a career, or even just a hobby, you can experience "pure knowledge" flowing unto you from the Spirit—about *any* subject. This divine help "shall greatly enlarge [your] soul" (D&C 121:42) in ways that you could never experience on your own.

Truly, "the glory of God is intelligence" (D&C 93:36), and His Spirit is always ready to help you gain, retain, and apply knowledge—whether it be spiritual or temporal.

Liken to Yourself

- What's a point of doctrine or a part of the scriptures that you have a hard time understanding? How could you involve the Spirit in helping you better understand that?
- What's something you would like to gain a stronger testimony about? Consider studying this topic more in depth and asking Heavenly Father to send His Spirit to confirm its truth to you.
- What kind of temporal knowledge do you stand in need of—for example, in your education or career? How do you think the Spirit can help you with this?

67. Russell M. Nelson, "What Will You Choose?," *Ensign*, Jan. 2015, 32.

L

Fills You with God's **Love**

"The love of God is shed abroad in our hearts by the Holy Ghost which is given unto us." (Romans 5:5)

This Will Help When . . .

- You're doubting your self-worth and God's love for you.
- You want to experience greater charity toward others.

Overview

"God's love" can be interpreted two different ways. First, it's the love possessed by God that He feels for His children. And second, it's a godly love, characteristic of Heavenly Father, that He blesses us to feel for others. The Holy Ghost can fill you with both types of love—especially in the moments you need it the most.

For example, think about "times of darkness, challenge, sorrow, or sin."[68] In these difficult moments, Satan may try to convince you that you are alone, unloved, worthless, forgotten, or hopeless. But consider these powerful words from President Thomas S. Monson:

68. Robert D. Hales, "Coming to Ourselves: The Sacrament, the Temple, and Sacrifice in Service," *Ensign* or *Liahona*, May 2012, 34.

> Your Heavenly Father loves you—each of you. That love never changes. It is not influenced by your appearance, by your possessions, or by the amount of money you have in your bank account. It is not changed by your talents and abilities. It is simply there. It is there for you when you are sad or happy, discouraged or hopeful. God's love is there for you whether or not you feel you deserve love. It is simply always there.
>
> As we seek our Heavenly Father through fervent, sincere prayer and earnest, dedicated scripture study . . . we will know of God's love for us. We will understand that we do not ever walk alone. I promise you that you will one day stand aside and look at your difficult times, and you will realize that He was always there beside you.[69]

This divine, incredible love is communicated to us through the Holy Ghost, who is "the messenger and revealer of the Father and the Son."[70] If you reach out to God—even when everything seems dark and it's the last thing you feel like doing—He will "encircle [you] about eternally in the arms of his love" (2 Nephi 1:15) and remind you of your eternal worth.

Now think of times when you especially need to feel love for *others*. Perhaps it's when you're faced with people "that curse you . . . hate you . . . despitefully use you, [or] persecute you" (Matthew 5:44). Or it could be when you're feeling "the spirit of contention . . . and [the devil] stirreth up [your heart] to contend with anger" (3 Nephi 11:29). Or maybe you're just having a bad day and feeling totally opposite the definition of charity found in Moroni 7:45—impatient, focused on yourself, irritable, and unable to bear the stress that burdens you.

Again, turning to God may be the last thing you feel like doing in moments like this. But the best solution—and what Heavenly Father wants you to do—is to "pray unto the Father with all the

---

69. Thomas S. Monson, "We Never Walk Alone," *Ensign* or *Liahona*, Nov. 2013, 123–124.
70. "Do Members of The Church of Jesus Christ of Latter-day Saints Believe in the Trinity?" ComeUntoChrist.org.

energy of heart, that ye may be filled with this love" (Moroni 7:48). If you do so, He will send you His Spirit, which "inspires virtue, kindness, goodness, tenderness, gentleness, and charity."[71] And through the Spirit, "Heavenly Father will help [you] love even those [you] may think are unlovable"[72]—including yourself.

Always remember that "God is love; and he that dwelleth in love dwelleth in God, and God in him" (1 John 4:16). The way we can tell "that we dwell in him, and he in us, [is] because he hath given us of his Spirit" (1 John 4:13), which fills us with His matchless love.

Liken to Yourself

- How does God manifest His love to you? What gets in the way of you feeling His love, and how can you overcome these obstacles?
- Who do you interact with most in your day-to-day life? What can you do to increase your love for these people—and also express it better?

---

71. Parley P. Pratt, *Key to the Science of Theology,* 4th ed. (1877), 102.
72. Neill F. Marriott, "Abiding in God and Repairing the Breach," *Ensign* or *Liahona*, Nov. 2017, 12.

M

Assists You in **Missionary** Work

"As the Lord's servant, you are to do His work in His way and by His power. . . . Rely on the Spirit rather than your own talents and abilities. Trust the Spirit to guide you in every aspect of your work." (Preach My Gospel)[73]

This Will Help When . . .

- You want to find people to share the gospel with.
- You're hesitant to share the gospel because you're not sure what to say or do.
- You fear rejection and opposition while doing missionary work.

Overview

In *The Power of Everyday Missionaries*, Clayton M. Christensen gives an excellent metaphor regarding missionary work and shares his own experience of being an active member missionary:

> In a war, the generals give the state-of-the-art weapons to those soldiers who are on the front lines engaged in direct combat with the enemy. To those of their troops who work

73. *Preach My Gospel: A Guide to Missionary Service* (2018), 97.

> in administrative positions behind the lines, they'll give less-potent tools. . . .
>
> [When I became] an active missionary again, I had essentially repositioned myself onto the front lines in the war against Satan over the souls of men. . . . The image in my mind is that God, my General, stands at the door when I go out every morning; and, knowing what the war is like, day after day He gives me His most powerful weapon: His Spirit.[74]

Truly, the Holy Ghost can help you in all aspects of missionary work—before, during, and after moments of preaching the gospel.

First, the Spirit "will guide you to people who will receive the message of the Restoration."[75] This can happen in so many ways. For example, if you keep a copy of the Book of Mormon with you and pray for an opportunity to share it, the Spirit can put you in the path of someone you can give it to and share your testimony with. But more often than not, missionary moments will happen not with strangers but with people you're acquainted with—neighbors, coworkers, relatives, old friends, current friends, and so on. With today's technology—especially the ability to connect with acquaintances through social media—the possibilities are pretty much endless. If you pray for revelation, the Spirit will prompt you with ideas about who you can share the good news of the gospel with.

Second, you can be "led by the Spirit to say what the Lord would have you say at just the right moment."[76] Honestly, many of us hesitate to seek out missionary opportunities because we're not sure what to say or do when they come. But in Doctrine and Covenants 84:85, the Lord gives us this comforting promise: "Neither take ye thought beforehand what ye shall say; but treasure up in your minds continually the words of life, and it shall be

---

74. Clayton M. Christensen, *The Power of Everyday Missionaries: The What and How of Sharing the Gospel* (2013), 4–5.
75. *Preach My Gospel* (2018), 89.
76. Ibid., 4.

given you in the very hour that portion that shall be meted unto every man."

As you're teaching people the gospel and inviting them to learn more, the Holy Ghost will help you know what to say and how to say it. And if you, like most people, are a bit nervous about doing missionary work, the Spirit can give you confidence and peace as you strive to do your best. As mentioned in the beginning of this section, God will not leave you to stand alone on the front lines in the war over the souls of men—He "will impart unto you of [His] Spirit, which shall enlighten your mind . . . [and] fill your soul with joy" (D&C 11:13).

Lastly, as you share eternal truths with other people, "the Holy Ghost shall be shed forth in bearing record unto all things whatsoever ye shall say" (D&C 100:8). It should take a load off your shoulders to know that, when all is said and done, the *Spirit* is the source of conversion—not you. Your role is to teach, testify, and invite; the Spirit's role is to carry the message "unto the hearts of the children of men" (2 Nephi 33:1); and the recipient's role is to choose whether to accept or reject it. Do your part, trust in the Spirit to do His part, and continue to pray and hope that others will accept the gospel message.

This role of the Spirit in conversion is also important for another reason—He can spiritually sustain you as you encounter opposition and rejection. Let's face it: It's not easy to deal with rejection, especially when it's your most sacredly held beliefs that are being rejected. You may even find yourself questioning certain aspects of the gospel as you listen to other people's questions and doubts. However, if you strive to keep the Holy Ghost with you, He will continually testify to you of the truth of the gospel, leaving you with an even firmer testimony than before.

Take heart in the Lord's promise to those who proclaim the gospel: "Whoso receiveth you, there I will be also, for I will go before your face. I will be on your right hand and on your left, and my Spirit shall be in your hearts, and mine angels round about you, to bear you up" (D&C 84:88).

Liken to Yourself

- How has the Holy Ghost helped you with missionary work in the past?
- Write a list of people you could potentially share the gospel with. As you try to listen to the Spirit, which names stand out to you the most? What could you do to help those people come unto Christ?
- What scares you the most about doing missionary work? How do you think the Spirit can help you overcome these concerns?

N

Helps You Put off the **Natural** Man

"For the natural man is an enemy to God,
and has been from the fall of Adam,
and will be, forever and ever, unless he yields
to the enticings of the Holy Spirit, and putteth off
the natural man and becometh a saint
through the atonement of Christ the Lord."
(Mosiah 3:19)

This Will Help When . . .

- You're struggling to overcome a weakness.
- You know you need to repent of a certain sin but are hesitant to forsake it.
- You want to be better at recognizing and resisting temptation.

Overview

As mortals, all of us have natural tendencies that are contrary to the laws and character of God. As you think about what the "natural man [or woman]" entails within yourself, consider these common attributes: "The natural man is . . . preoccupied with the rewards of this world, . . . yields himself to the harsh and the crude,"[77] and is characterized by "selfishness, pride, anger, and incivility."[78] Now compare that with the saintly qualities found in Mosiah 3:19: "submissive, meek, humble, patient, full of love, willing to submit to all things which the Lord seeth fit to inflict upon him." That's quite a contrast!

Sometimes it can be disheartening to look at this spectrum, see where you are, and see how far you still need to go. But this is exactly why God gave you this life! As Elder David A. Bednar explained:

> The precise nature of the test of mortality, then, can be summarized in the following question: Will I respond to the inclinations of the natural man, or will I yield to the enticings of the Holy Spirit and put off the natural man and become a saint through the Atonement of Christ the Lord? That is the test. Every appetite, desire, propensity, and impulse of the natural man may be overcome by and through the Atonement of Jesus Christ. We are here on the earth to develop godlike qualities and to bridle all of the passions of the flesh.[79]

Now let's look at a few ways the Holy Ghost can help you in this lifelong quest of spiritual transformation and sanctification.

First, the Spirit will encourage you to repent—not just "someday" but *now*. It can be very difficult to forsake a sin, especially when it brings temporal pleasure and the natural man wants to delay repentance as much as possible. But as the *For the Strength of Youth* booklet teaches, "The sooner you repent, the sooner you begin to make your way back and find the peace and joy that come with forgiveness."[80] To assist with this, the Spirit can help you see the benefits of forsaking a sin versus the consequences of continuing

---

77. Robert L. Millet, "Putting Off the Natural Man: 'An Enemy to God'," *Ensign*, June 1992.
78. *Preparing for an Eternal Marriage Teacher Manual* (2003), 31.
79. Elder David A. Bednar, "We Believe in Being Chaste," *Ensign* or *Liahona*, May 2013, 43.
80. *For the Strength of Youth* (booklet, 2011), 28.

in it. Also, the closer your relationship is with the Holy Ghost, the quicker you'll notice His departure when you sin—and the sooner you'll want to repent to bring Him back.

Second, the Spirit can point out to you the blessings that come from yielding to His enticings rather than Satan's temptations. You may have to deal with certain weaknesses your entire life, and it may *always* be difficult to resist those inclinations. However, one way the Lord will help you endure is by revealing to you the blessings of righteousness. This includes the blessings you experience *now* because of your righteousness, as well as the blessings you'll experience in *eternity* if you continue faithful. As 1 Corinthians 2:9–10 teaches, "Eye hath not seen, nor ear heard, neither have entered into the heart of man, the things which God hath prepared for them that love him. But God hath revealed them unto us *by his Spirit*" (emphasis added). Knowing of such blessings will surely give you the motivation you need as you seek to put off the natural man.

Lastly, the Spirit can help you resist temptation when ungodly desires come along. As the New Testament teaches, God "will not suffer you to be tempted above that ye are able; but will with the temptation also make a way to escape, that ye may be able to bear it" (1 Corinthians 10:13). The Spirit will help you recognize temptations for what they are, give you the strength to resist or escape from them, and help you avoid them in the first place. And, as President Henry B. Eyring said, "The companionship of the Holy Ghost makes what is good more attractive and temptation less compelling. That alone should be enough to make us determined to qualify for the Spirit to be with us always."[81]

The whole purpose of the gospel is "to make bad [people] good and good [people] better, and to change human nature." [82] The Spirit is vital in this process because, as C. S. Lewis once noted, "Everything which really needs to be done in our souls can be done

---

81. Henry B. Eyring, "The Holy Ghost as Your Companion," *Ensign* or *Liahona*, Nov. 2015, 104.
82. See Franklin D. Richards, in Conference Report, Oct. 1965, 136–37; see also David O. McKay, in Conference Report, Apr. 1954, 26.

only by God."[83] As you work with the Holy Ghost and continually yield to His enticings, you can personally experience a "transformative rebirth" [84] and all the blessings that come with putting off the natural man.

Liken to Yourself

- When you think of what the "natural man [or woman]" means within yourself personally, what comes to mind? What progress have you made so far in putting off your natural urges, and what progress would you like to make next?
- What blessings have you experienced as you've followed "the enticings of the Holy Spirit" (Mosiah 3:19) instead of the enticings of Satan?
- What are your biggest temptations at the moment? How can you increase the influence of the Spirit in your life to help you resist these temptations?

---

83. C. S. Lewis, *Mere Christianity* (1996), 166.
84. D. Todd Christofferson, "Born Again," *Ensign* or *Liahona*, May 2008, 77.

O

Opens Your Spiritual Eyes

"By the power of the Spirit our eyes were opened and our understandings were enlightened, so as to see and understand the things of God." (D&C 76:12)

This Will Help When . . .

- You feel overwhelmed by temporal concerns.
- You're having a hard time keeping an eternal perspective.
- You want to see others and yourself as God does.

Overview

As we go throughout our lives, it's not always easy for us to see things the way God sees them. Rather, it's as if "we see through a glass, darkly" (1 Corinthians 13:12), often focusing on the temporal far more than the spiritual. However, with the help of the Holy Ghost, "our eyes [can be] opened and our understandings [can be] enlightened, so as to see and understand the things of God" (D&C 76:12).

For example, the Holy Ghost can help you keep an eternal perspective, especially in times of trial. President Spencer W. Kimball wrote the following:

> If we looked at mortality as the whole of existence, then pain, sorrow, failure, and short life would be calamity. But if we look upon life as an eternal thing stretching far into the premortal past and on into the eternal post-death future, then all happenings may be put in proper perspective.[85]

When you remember that "this life is the time for men to prepare to meet God" (Alma 34:32), you can see trials for what they really are—tests that prove and refine your character. Then, suddenly you realize that financial hardship is simply a test of humility, diligence, and perseverance. Family problems become a test of charity, patience, and forgiveness. And, ultimately, every trial becomes an opportunity to deepen your trust in God, refine your character, and practice receiving and following revelation.

You may not think a simple change in perspective would do much to alleviate the pain of trials, but as Victor Frankl wrote, "Suffering ceases to be suffering at the moment it finds a meaning."[86] When you give your trials meaning—which the Spirit can help you do—you truly realize that "all these things shall give thee experience, and shall be for thy good" (D&C 122:7).

Another way the Holy Ghost can open your spiritual eyes is by helping you see the divine worth in people. Elder Dale G. Renlund taught:

> To effectively serve others we must see them through a parent's eyes, through Heavenly Father's eyes. Only then can we begin to comprehend the true worth of a soul. Only then can we sense the love that Heavenly Father has for all of His children.[87]

As the Spirit helps you see people "not as they are but as they can become,"[88] He will also help you see *yourself* in that light. And

---

85. *Teachings of Presidents of the Church: Spencer W. Kimball* (2006), 15.
86. Viktor Frankl, *Man's Search for Meaning* (2006), 113.
87. Dale G. Renlund, "Through God's Eyes," *Ensign* or *Liahona*, Nov. 2015, 94.
88. Thomas S. Monson, "See Others as They May Become," *Ensign* or *Liahona*, Nov. 2012, 70.

"remembering who you are—a child of God with infinite worth—[will give] you the assurance that your all-powerful Father in Heaven is willing and wanting and waiting to help you."[89]

While it's true that "[God's] thoughts are not your thoughts" (Isaiah 55:8), with the help of the Spirit they *can* be. "The eyes of your understanding [can be] enlightened" (Ephesians 1:18), so that you see things the way God sees them and can therefore act in a more godlike way. Jesus once said to His disciples, "Blessed are your eyes, for they see" (Matthew 13:16). When you allow the Spirit to open your spiritual eyes to see, truly you will be blessed to know "the mysteries and peaceable things—that which bringeth joy, that which bringeth life eternal" (D&C 42:61).

Liken to Yourself

- What does it mean to you to have an eternal perspective? Consider the endeavors and activities you're currently pursuing in your life. How does the meaning of these things change as you view them with an eternal perspective?
- Consider the trials you're going through right now. What do you think the Lord wants you to learn from them? What experience are you gaining that will help you in the future—both in this life and in eternity?
- How well do you see others—and yourself—as God does? How could you improve?

89. Jean B. Bingham, "Keys to Progress: An Eternal Perspective" (Brigham Young University–Idaho devotional, Nov. 27, 2018), byui.edu.

P

Brings You **Peace**

"Peace I leave with you, my peace I give unto you: not as the world giveth, give I unto you. Let not your heart be troubled, neither let it be afraid." (John 14:27)

This Will Help When . . .

- You feel troubled about the problems happening in the world or in your personal life.
- You're experiencing feelings of fear and worry.
- You'd like to find greater peace in your life.

Overview

We live in a time when "peace has been taken from the earth"[90]—a time in which "the whole earth shall be in commotion, and men's hearts shall fail them" (D&C 45:26). However, there is a peace that you can have in your heart despite any chaos, instability, or calamities happening in the world—or even in your personal life. It is "the inner calm and comfort born of the Spirit that God gives to His faithful Saints."[91] In other words, "even if all the world is

90. Ezra Taft Benson, "A Voice of Warning," *Ensign*, Jan. 1993.
91. Guide to the Scriptures, "Peace," scriptures.ChurchofJesusChrist.org.

crumbling around [you], the promised Comforter will provide His peace as a result of true discipleship."[92]

The biggest problem is that when we're feeling unsettled and we ask ourselves "Where can I turn for peace?"[93], it's not always God that we turn to. Think about it for a moment. What "other sources" do you turn to for peace, but which ultimately "cease to make [you] whole"[94]? Perhaps you numb yourself with time-wasting media, indulge in unhealthy food, or distract yourself with a never-ending barrage of tasks.

Whatever worldly solution you come up with, try to catch yourself in that moment and remember who the ultimate source of comfort is—the Savior Jesus Christ, the true Prince of Peace. For He clearly taught, "Learn of me, and listen to my words; walk in the meekness of my Spirit, and *you shall have peace in me*" (D&C 19:23; emphasis added). As you seek the companionship of the Holy Ghost, especially in times of anguish, you will discover the truth of President James E. Faust's words: "The Spirit of the Holy Ghost is the greatest guarantor of inward peace in our unstable world. It can be more mind-expanding and can make us have a better sense of well-being than any chemical or other earthly substance. It will calm nerves; it will breathe peace to our souls."[95]

A common enemy of peace is fear. Consider just a few examples listed by Elder Ronald A. Rasband:

> Our single adults fear making commitments such as getting married. Young marrieds . . . fear bringing children into an increasingly wicked world. Missionaries fear lots of things, especially approaching strangers. Widows fear going forward alone. Teenagers fear not being accepted;

---

92. Dennis E. Simmons, "His Peace," *Ensign*, May 1997.
93. "Where Can I Turn for Peace?," *Hymns*, no. 129.
94. Ibid.
95. James E. Faust, "The Gift of the Holy Ghost—A Sure Compass," *Ensign*, May 1989.

> grade schoolers fear the first day of school; university students fear getting back a test. We fear failure, rejection, disappointment, and the unknown. We fear hurricanes, earthquakes, and fires that ravage the land and our lives. We fear not being chosen, and on the flip side, we fear being chosen. We fear not being good enough; we fear that the Lord has no blessings for us. We fear change, and our fears can escalate to terror.[96]

Elder Rasband goes on to explain that fear can be dispelled with the help of the Holy Ghost, especially as we seek Him in holy places. "Our desire to 'always have his Spirit' [Moroni 4:3] with us will push fear aside for a more eternal view of our mortal lives. . . . When we stand in holy places . . . we feel the Spirit of the Lord with us. We find answers to questions that trouble us or the peace to simply set them aside. . . . We can feel God's love, and 'perfect love casteth out all fear' [Moroni 8:16]."[97]

So, the next time you feel a lack of peace, reach out to the Lord and seek the Holy Ghost—and They will help you. As the lyrics of "Where Can I Turn for Peace?" eloquently express:

> [The Lord] answers privately,
> Reaches my reaching
> In my Gethsemane, Savior and Friend.
> Gentle the peace he finds for my beseeching.
> Constant he is and kind,
> Love without end.

Liken to Yourself

- When you feel troubled, what worldly sources do you tend to turn to for peace, and why? What can you do to seek the Prince of Peace instead?

---

96. Ronald A. Rasband, "Be Not Troubled," *Ensign* or *Liahona*, Nov. 2018, 18.
97. Ibid., 19.

- What things do you worry about or fear the most? Consider expressing these concerns to God in prayer, and pay attention to the thoughts and feelings the Spirit gives you in response.
- How can you follow Elder Rasband's advice to "stand in holy places"? How have you been blessed by doing so in the past?

Q

Quickens Your Physical Body

"[God] shall also quicken your mortal bodies by his Spirit that dwelleth in you." (Romans 8:11)

This Will Help When . . .

- You want to be healthier.
- You are dealing with pain, sickness, or other physical difficulties.
- You sometimes need a boost of physical or mental energy to accomplish a task.

Overview

The word *quicken* means "to make alive" or "to give life or energy to." Now, we usually think of the Holy Ghost as giving *spiritual* life and energy, but did you know He can also bless you *physically*? Consider the words of Parley P. Pratt:

> The Holy Ghost . . . quickens all the intellectual faculties, increases, enlarges, expands and purifies all the natural passions and affections. . . . It develops beauty of person, form and features. It tends to health, vigor, animation, and social feeling. It invigorates all the faculties of the physical and intellectual man. It strengthens, and gives tone to the nerves. In short, it is, as it were, marrow to the bone, joy to

> the heart, light to the eyes, music to the ears, and life to the whole being.[98]

This quote helps us to see that the word *strengthen* in the gospel shouldn't just be limited to a spiritual interpretation. In other words, don't underestimate God's ability to strengthen you physically when needed. After all, a great deal of our lives depends on our physical health and stamina, not just our spiritual well-being.

For example, as Nephi reflected on his family's travels in the wilderness—something that surely required both spiritual *and* physical strength—he noted that "so great were the blessings of the Lord upon us, that while we did live upon raw meat in the wilderness, our women did give plenty of suck for their children, and were strong, yea, even like unto the men" (1 Nephi 17:2). Then he testified, "If it so be that the children of men keep the commandments of God he doth *nourish* them, and *strengthen* them, and provide means whereby they can accomplish the thing which he has commanded them" (1 Nephi 17:3; emphasis added). Clearly, this nourishment and strength wasn't just spiritual in nature.

As another, more modern example, consider this experience shared by Elder M. Russell Ballard:

> Recently I was alone in my office. I had just gone through a medical procedure on my hand. It was black and blue, swollen, and it was painful. As I sat at my desk, I could not focus on important and critical matters because I was distracted by this pain. I knelt in prayer and asked the Lord to help me focus so I could accomplish my work. I stood and returned to the pile of papers on my desk. Almost immediately, clarity and focus came to my mind, and I was able to complete the pressing matters before me.[99]

As you pray for the needed strength and energy to do the tasks that lay before you, that "clarity and focus" can come to you too

98. Parley P. Pratt, *Key to the Science of Theology,* 9th ed. (1965), 101.
99. M. Russell Ballard, "Watch Ye Therefore, and Pray Always," *Ensign* or *Liahona*, Nov. 2020, 79.

through the power of the Spirit. The Holy Ghost can help you endure pain, think clearly when your mind feels foggy, keep moving forward when your body is weak, and perform to the best of your physical abilities. As President George Albert Smith taught, "The companionship of the spirit of the Lord is an antidote for weariness."[100]

Because "the spirit and the body are the soul of man" (D&C 88:15), it makes sense that the Spirit can invigorate you both spiritually and physically. However, this is a two-way street, meaning that if you want to maximize the Spirit in your life, you need to also take care of your *body* and not just your spirit. Elder Jörg Klebingat gave this counsel:

> Feeding the spirit while neglecting the body, which is a temple, usually leads to spiritual dissonance. . . . President Boyd K. Packer has taught "that our spirit and our body are combined in such a way that our body becomes an instrument of our mind and the foundation of our character." Therefore, please use good judgment in what and especially how much you eat, and regularly give your body the exercise it needs and deserves. If you are physically able, decide today to be the master of your own house and begin a regular, long-term exercise program, suited to your abilities, combined with a healthier diet. Spiritual confidence increases when your spirit, with the help of the Savior, is truly in charge of your natural man or woman.[101]

As you seek to take care of both your body and spirit, the Holy Ghost will surely bless you with "health in [your] navel and marrow to [your] bones. . . . And [you] shall run and not be weary, and shall walk and not faint" (D&C 89:18, 20).

---

100. *Teachings of Presidents of the Church: George Albert Smith* (2011), 119.
101. Jörg Klebingat, "Approaching the Throne of God with Confidence," *Ensign* or *Liahona*, Nov. 2014, 35.

Liken to Yourself

- What health challenges do you have, if any? In what ways do you need to be physically strengthened in order to perform your daily tasks? Ask Heavenly Father in prayer to give you the physical energy you stand in need of, and listen to the promptings of the Spirit to know how you can improve your physical health.
- What could you begin doing this week to follow the counsel of Elder Klebingat in regard to a healthy diet and regular exercise? Also, what can you do to make sure you're getting enough sleep (as well as not oversleeping)?

R

Helps You **Remember**

"The Holy Ghost, whom the Father will send in my name, he shall teach you all things, and bring all things to your remembrance, whatsoever I have said unto you." (John 14:26)

This Will Help When . . .

- You want to be a more powerful gospel teacher.
- You'd like to better remember the spiritual experiences you've had in the past.
- You sometimes need to recall information (spiritual or non-spiritual) in a moment of need.

Overview

President Spencer W. Kimball believed that the most important word in the dictionary could be *remember*.[102] And President Henry B. Eyring taught that "remembering may be one of the most precious gifts the Spirit can give you."[103] Let's take a look

102. Referenced in Henry B. Eyring, "Always Remember Him," *Ensign*, Feb. 2018, 4.
103. Henry B. Eyring, "'My Peace I Leave with You'," *Ensign* or *Liahona*, May 2017, 16.

at what the Holy Ghost can help you remember and how it can bless your life.

First, the Spirit can help you draw from a deep reservoir of knowledge and wisdom when teaching the gospel—whether that be to a nonmember, at church, or in your family. This is why the Lord counsels, "Neither take ye thought beforehand what ye shall say; but treasure up in your minds continually the words of life, and it shall be given you in the very hour that portion that shall be meted unto every man" (D&C 84:85).

Now, that doesn't mean you can get away with just "winging it" when you give a talk in church or lead a family home evening lesson. Those should certainly be planned in advance. But it does mean that your greatest tool in becoming a powerful gospel teacher is to consistently immerse yourself in gospel study, "treasure these things up in your hearts, and let the solemnities of eternity rest upon your minds" (D&C 43:34). Then, as you plan and teach those lessons—and when unexpected teaching opportunities come along—the Spirit will "bring all things to your remembrance" (John 14:26), drawing from a deep well that you have already filled to the brim with knowledge and wisdom.

Second, the Holy Ghost can help you remember spiritual experiences that you've had in the past, which is particularly important during trials of faith. President Henry B. Eyring taught:

> You will at times have your faith challenged by Satan; it happens to all disciples of Jesus Christ. Your defense against these attacks is to keep the Holy Ghost as your companion. . . . He will bring back the memory of those times when you felt the light and the love of Jesus Christ. . . . The memory may be of an answered prayer, of a priesthood ordinance received, of a confirmation of your testimony, or of a moment when you saw God's guiding hand in your life.[104]

Elder Jeffrey R. Holland likewise counseled us to not "draw back" when doubts arise, choosing instead to remember the

104. Henry B. Eyring, "'My Peace I Leave with You'," 16.

"moments of revelation and conviction [that] have given us a peace and an assurance we thought we would never lose." He urges, "Don't lose your confidence. Don't forget how you once felt. Don't distrust the experience you had. That tenacity is what saved Moses when the adversary confronted him, and it is what will save you."[105]

The Holy Ghost can bring such memories of conviction to the forefront of your mind, giving you the confidence you need to push through the darkness of doubt. This way, you can continually renew your testimony and zeal for the gospel, which is what Alma was encouraging when he asked, "If ye have experienced a change of heart, and if ye have felt to sing the song of redeeming love, I would ask, can ye feel so now?" (Alma 5:26) With the help of the Holy Ghost bringing past spiritual experiences to your remembrance—as well as giving you new spiritual experiences—you can answer "Yes!" to that question today, tomorrow, and forever.

Lastly, the Spirit can help you recall temporal (non-spiritual) information. As discussed in the chapter about knowledge, "all things unto [God] are spiritual" (D&C 29:34), and the Holy Ghost can help with temporal matters just as much as with spiritual ones. Therefore, if you continually fill the reservoir of your mind with knowledge and skills pertaining to your field of education or work, the Holy Ghost can help you retain them and recall them when needed.

Like President Eyring said, remembering "is one of the most precious gifts the Spirit can give you." And similarly, one of the most precious gifts you can give God is to remember—specifically to remember His Son, Jesus Christ. You are promised in the sacrament prayers that if you "are willing to take upon [you] the name of [Jesus Christ], and *always remember him*, and keep his commandments . . . [you] may always have his Spirit to be with [you]" (Moroni 4:3; emphasis added). In other words, as you seek to remember the Savior, you will be blessed with the companionship

105. Jeffrey R. Holland, "'Cast Not Away Therefore Your Confidence'" (Brigham Young University devotional, Mar. 2, 1999), speeches.byu.edu.

of the Holy Ghost—and the Spirit will in turn help you to remember everything else that is important and necessary.

Liken to Yourself

- How can you improve your gospel study in order to "treasure up in your [mind] continually the words of life" (D&C 84:85)? Write down a plan of what to study, when, and how to make it most effective for you.
- When you think about powerful spiritual experiences you've had in your life, what does the Spirit bring to mind? If you've written about them somewhere, go back and reread them. If not, consider writing them down in a journal.
- When do you most need to recall knowledge, whether it be temporal or spiritual? How can you involve the Holy Ghost more during those times?

S

Empowers Your **Scripture** Study

"Angels speak by the power of the Holy Ghost; wherefore, they speak the words of Christ. Wherefore . . . feast upon the words of Christ; for . . . [they] will tell you all things what ye should do." (2 Nephi 32:3)

This Will Help When . . .

- You want to improve your gospel study.
- You have a hard time understanding the scriptures and how they apply to you.
- You get bored studying the same gospel topics and scriptures over and over again.

Overview

Scripture study is a key part of gospel living, and the companionship of the Holy Ghost is a key part of effective scripture study. As President Dallin H. Oaks once taught, "The word of the Lord in the scriptures is like a lamp to guide our feet (see Psalm 119:105), and revelation is like a mighty force that increases the lamp's illumination manyfold."[106]

---

106. Dallin H. Oaks, "Scripture Reading and Revelation," *Ensign*, Jan. 1995.

The Spirit can empower your scripture study in several ways. For example, the Holy Ghost can help you understand scriptures that are difficult to comprehend. Let's be honest—it's not always easy to understand things that were written thousands of years ago and mostly in a distant land. To help with this, we need to follow the Lord's counsel to "seek learning, even by study and also by faith" (D&C 88:118). Here, "by study" could be interpreted as your *own* efforts to understand the scriptures, and "by faith" could imply inviting the *Spirit* to teach you through revelation.

When it comes to putting forth personal effort, the Church has countless resources—most that are available at the click of a button—that can help you understand the background, context, and importance of confusing passages. And as for revelation, God most certainly knows the meaning behind all of His words, so He can communicate that to you through His Spirit as you prayerfully study. Thus, "by study and also by faith," you'll be able to comprehend and find personal meaning in even the most obscure scriptural passages. Just as Joseph Smith used the Urim and Thummin to translate the Book of Mormon into English, so too can the Holy Ghost translate confusing scriptures into a language you understand.

Second, the Spirit can guide you to exactly what you need when you need it. There are countless stories of people being led to that "perfect scripture" in a time of need—and you may have experienced this yourself. But perhaps the reason this kind of occurrence happens so often isn't because of the scriptures themselves but rather that the Spirit is capable of drawing meaning out of practically any scripture. *And* He can powerfully communicate that meaning to you personally, applying it to your particular situation. In this way, "scripture study becomes the channel for the Spirit to give each of us a customized tutorial."[107] Comparing the word of God to the Liahona, the Holy Ghost is truly the one spinning the spindles that "[point] the way whither we should go" (1 Nephi 16:10).

---

107. C. Scott Grow, "And This Is Life Eternal," *Ensign* or *Liahona*, May 2017, 122.

Lastly, the Holy Ghost can help you continually find new meaning and application in scriptures you've already read and know well. Heraclitus, an ancient Greek philosopher, once said, "No man ever steps in the same river twice, for it's not the same river and he's not the same man."[108] Likewise, you should never tire of immersing yourself in the scriptures because (1) "many of the prophecies and doctrinal passages in the scriptures have multiple meanings,"[109] and (2) you are a different person every time you read them—facing different trials and in need of different counsel. This is the reason "we are encouraged to read the scriptures again and again. By this means, we obtain access to what our Heavenly Father would have us know and do in our personal lives *today*."[110] God will communicate that to you through the Spirit—no matter how many times you've previously read the scriptures.

Prayerfully studying the scriptures is a sure way to invite the Spirit into your life, and having the Spirit guide your scripture study is a sure way to "open doors of revelation"[111] to learn what God would have you know. You will be deeply blessed by heeding the following counsel, given by President Dieter F. Uchtdorf:

> In our learning, let us not neglect the fountain of revelation. The scriptures and the words of modern-day apostles and prophets are the sources of wisdom, divine knowledge, and personal revelation to help us find answers to all the challenges in life. Let us learn of Christ; let us seek out that knowledge which leads to peace, truth, and the sublime mysteries of eternity.[112]

---

108. See, for example, https://www.brainyquote.com/quotes/heraclitus_107157.
109. Dallin H. Oaks, "Scripture Reading and Revelation."
110. Ibid., emphasis added.
111. James B. Martino, "Turn to Him and Answers Will Come," *Ensign* or *Liahona*, Nov. 2015, 59.
112. Dieter F. Uchtdorf, "Two Principles for Any Economy," *Ensign* or *Liahona*, Nov. 2009, 58.

Liken to Yourself

- How has the Holy Ghost helped you with scripture study in the past, and how would you like Him to help you now?
- What are you currently studying in the scriptures? What resources could you use to better understand the background, context, and meaning of those scriptures?
- What can you do to increase the presence of the Spirit during your scripture study?

T

Reveals the **Truth** of All Things

"And by the power of the Holy Ghost ye may know the truth of all things." (Moroni 10:5)

This Will Help When . . .

- You want to develop a deeper testimony of the gospel.
- You want to better distinguish between truth and error—both in the world and within your own thinking patterns.

Overview

While speaking with Jesus Christ before His crucifixion, Pontius Pilate asked a pertinent question: "What is truth?" (John 18:38) President Dieter F. Uchtdorf expounded on this, saying, "I sense a certain weary cynicism in Pilate's reply. . . . I wonder if what he really was asking was 'How can anyone possibly know the truth?'"[113] The answer to that question is by the power of the Holy Ghost, for "the Spirit . . . will guide you into all truth" (John 16:13).

A central mission of the Holy Ghost is to testify of the truth of the gospel of Jesus Christ. This is certainly the case for those

113. Dieter F. Uchtdorf, "What Is Truth?" (Brigham Young University devotional, Jan. 13, 2013), speeches.byu.edu.

investigating the Church, which is why missionaries consistently ask people to "experiment upon [their] words" (Alma 32:27). They understand that through reading the scriptures, praying, and keeping the commandments, investigators will "gain [a] divine witness from the Holy Spirit"[114] that the Church is true.

However, the Spirit's testifying power isn't just for investigators—it's for all of us. Elder Craig C. Christensen taught the following:

> Some people speak of a testimony as if it were a light switch—it's either on or off; you either have a testimony, or you do not. In reality, a testimony is more like a tree that passes through various stages of growth and development. . . . [Our testimonies] grow and develop over time through constant nourishment and frequent spiritual encounters.[115]

The Holy Ghost can continually strengthen and renew your testimony. As Professor Robert L. Millet taught, "One cannot afford to coast spiritually, to live forevermore on past sacred moments; new ones must be sought for, treasured, and stored in our reservoir of faith."[116] In other words, your faith doesn't have to depend on hazy spiritual experiences from the distant past. It can be rooted in a continual stream of revelation. Then, in moments of doubt or troubling times, you'll be able to "hold fast to what you already know and stand strong until additional knowledge comes."[117]

Another important way the Spirit can assist you is by helping you discern between truth and error. This goes far beyond just the spiritual realm—the world is full of misinformation regarding just about everything. But as Elder Neal A. Maxwell put it, "Happily . . . the Holy Ghost not only helps us to recognize plain

---

114. Introduction to the Book of Mormon.
115. Craig C. Christensen, "I Know These Things of Myself," *Ensign* or *Liahona*, Nov. 2014, 51.
116. Robert L. Millet, *The Holy Spirit: His Identity, Mission, and Ministry* (2019), 226.
117. Jeffrey R. Holland, "'Lord, I Believe'," *Ensign* or *Liahona*, May 2013, 94.

truth but also plain nonsense!"[118] If you ever come across something you're not sure is true—whether that be a news story, an academic theory, a political assertion, or anything else—ask *God* if it's true. And when confronted with competing opinions about complex issues, ask God what *His* opinion is. In the simple words of James 1:5, "If any of you lack wisdom, let him ask of God, that giveth to all men liberally, and upbraideth not; and it shall be given him"—through the Holy Ghost. As you pray with faith, ponder with humility, and study with diligence, you will be able to distinguish between truth and error with the help of the Spirit.

Unfortunately, the world isn't the only source of misinformation you're up against. Oftentimes, we need to look no further than our own minds to find a war between truth and error. For example, President Ezra Taft Benson taught that "Satan is increasingly striving to overcome the Saints with despair, discouragement, despondency, and depression."[119] Such feelings are usually accompanied by thoughts such as "I'm worthless and helpless," "I fail at everything I do," "I'm so stupid," and "I'm never going to get this right." But are those statements *true*? No! Yet in the moment, it can be so hard to see that.

That's why it's crucial to stay close to the Spirit and allow Him into your heart and mind—because He "speaketh of things as they *really are*, and of things as they *really will be*" (Jacob 4:13; emphasis added). In other words, the Holy Ghost can help you recognize distortions of reality in your own mind. *And* He can help you reframe those thoughts to align with the truth. Your choruses of "I am a worthless failure" can be transformed into "I am a child of God—a very imperfect one, yes, but one whose worth is great in the sight of God."

In answer to Pilate's original question, the Lord defines truth as a "knowledge of things as they are, and as they were, and as they are to come" (D&C 93:24). And who can know it? Anyone who

---

118. Neal A. Maxwell, "'Behold, the Enemy Is Combined' (D&C 38:12)," *Ensign*, May 1993.
119. Ezra Taft Benson, "Do Not Despair," *Ensign*, Nov. 1974.

"[takes] the Holy Spirit for their guide" (D&C 45:57). Amidst all the questions and doubts—in a world that is "confusing and noisy, full of deception and distractions"[120]—"the Spirit is the only witness that is sure and certain and infallible."[121] What a miraculous gift from God, and one that is so needed in today's world.

Liken to Yourself

- In what ways do you think you need to strengthen your testimony? (For example, are there any doctrines you struggle to accept?) What are some specific things you could do to deepen your testimony in this area?
- What are some examples of competing messages in the world that people claim to be true? What is the Spirit telling you about what's actually true?
- What distorted thoughts do you tend to struggle with, and what's untrue about them? What truths do you think the Spirit wants you to internalize instead?

---

120. Milton Camargo, "Ask, Seek, and Knock," *Ensign* or *Liahona*, Nov. 2020, 107.
121. Tad R. Callister, "The Book of Mormon: Man-Made or God-Given?" (Brigham Young University devotional, Nov. 1, 2016), speeches.byu.edu.

U

Speaks to Your **Understanding**

"For the Lord God giveth light unto the understanding; for he speaketh unto men according to their language, unto their understanding." (2 Nephi 31:3)

This Will Help When . . .

- You want to better understand how the Spirit speaks to you personally.
- You worry that you don't feel the Holy Ghost the same way others do.

Overview

One of the most well-known scriptures about the Holy Ghost is Doctrine and Covenants 8:2, and this is usually how it's emphasized: "I will tell you in your *mind* and in your *heart*, by the Holy Ghost." But there's a different way to emphasize it as well: "I will tell you in *your* mind and in *your* heart." Your mind and heart are completely unique to *you*—the way you think, the way you feel, the way you look at the world and experience what you experience. Therefore, even though there are general principles of revelation that apply to everyone, the Spirit is still going to speak to you in a unique way—"according to [your] language, unto [your] understanding" (2 Nephi 31:3).

For example, Lehi experienced his prophetic call in a way consistent with other Israelite prophets at the time, including "seeing God upon His throne, seeing the heavenly hosts, [and] receiving a heavenly book."[122] God knew that this is how Lehi would understand best. Also, in this dispensation, the Lord used the words "the field is white already to harvest" (D&C 4:4) to communicate with Joseph Smith Sr., a farmer who would immediately recognize the significance of such imagery.

So, how does the Spirit reach and teach *you*?

If you have a hard time answering that question, don't despair. As Sister Linda K. Burton explained, "Just as learning an instrument or a language is a process, learning the language of the Spirit is also a process."[123] Additionally, President Russell M. Nelson taught that "it has never been more imperative to know how the Spirit speaks to you than right now. . . . I renew my plea for you to do *whatever* it takes to increase your spiritual capacity to receive personal revelation."[124] Hopefully this book helps you recognize when you've felt the Spirit in the past and gives you plenty of ideas on how to seek the Spirit in the future. And when in doubt, know that you can always ask God to help you understand how the Spirit communicates with you personally.

It's also worth mentioning that everyone feels the Spirit in a slightly different way, so you shouldn't be discouraged if you receive revelation differently than others. President Dallin H. Oaks shared this example:

> I have met persons who told me they have never had a witness from the Holy Ghost because they have never felt their bosom "burn within" them. What does a "burning in the bosom" mean [see D&C 9:8]? Does it need to be a feeling of caloric

---

122. "Why Does the Lord Speak to Men 'According to Their Language'?" BookOfMormonCentral.org.
123. Linda K. Burton, "Tuning Our Hearts to the Voice of the Spirit" (Church Educational System devotional for young adults, Mar. 2, 2014), broadcasts.ChurchofJesusChrist.org.
124. Russell M. Nelson, "Hear Him," *Ensign* or *Liahona*, May 2020, 90.

> heat, like the burning produced by combustion? If that is the meaning, I have never had a burning in the bosom. Surely, the word "burning" in this scripture signifies a feeling of comfort and serenity. That is the witness many receive. That is the way revelation works.[125]

To better understand the Holy Ghost, study the words of the prophets—ancient and modern. Their teachings are replete with doctrine about the Spirit and examples of how He has communicated with others. And, as mentioned before, study yourself. What hobbies, interests, or background do you have that the Spirit might reference as He teaches you? What role might your personality play in how He communicates with you? For example, if you're more of a logical thinker, perhaps the Spirit is more likely to help you make rational connections in your mind. If you're more sentimental, He may be more prone to give you feelings in your heart.

In any case, trust that the Holy Ghost will be able to get through to you in *some* way that you will understand and recognize. As the Savior taught, "When a man reasoneth he is understood of man. . . . Even so will I, the Lord, reason with you that you may understand" (D&C 50:12). And while you're in the process of learning the vital language of the Spirit, you can hold fast to this simple explanation by President Gordon B. Hinckley: "How do we recognize the promptings of the Spirit? I don't think that's too difficult, really. . . . Does it persuade one to do good, to rise, to stand tall, to do the right thing, to be kind, to be generous? Then it is of the Spirit of God."[126]

Liken to Yourself

- When was the last time you felt the Holy Ghost communicating with you, and what was that experience like?

125. Dallin H. Oaks, "Teaching and Learning by the Spirit," *Ensign*, Mar. 1997.
126. *Teachings of Presidents of the Church: Gordon B. Hinckley* (2016), 260–261.

- Look back at the questions in this chapter and ponder them: How does the Spirit reach and teach you? What hobbies, interests, or background do you have that the Spirit might reference as He teaches you? What role might your personality play in how He communicates with you?

V

Can Send You **Visions**

"In the last days, saith God, I will pour out of my Spirit upon all flesh . . . and your young men shall see visions, and your old men shall dream dreams." (Acts 2:17)

This Will Help When . . .

- You want to know how to determine whether a dream is from God or not.
- You want to find more spiritual meaning in your dreams.

Overview

When it comes to methods of revelation, many people consider dreams to be a thing of ancient times—like Pharaoh's dream warning him of famine (see Genesis 41), Joseph's dream instructing him to take Mary as his wife (see Matthew 1), and Lehi's dream of the tree of life (see 1 Nephi 8). But if it's true that "God is the same yesterday, today, and forever" (Mormon 9:9), it logically follows that spiritually significant dreams can still come to those who are worthy to receive them—including you. Simply put, "inspired dreams are the fruit of faith."[127]

127. Guide to the Scriptures, "Dream," scriptures.ChurchofJesusChrist.org.

Of course, not all dreams are from God. "Dreams are often nonsensical or downright weird, which can make us question whether any dream could ever really mean anything."[128] However, President Harold B. Lee warned of the tendency to dismiss dreams as always being void of divine inspiration: "I fear that there are those of us who are prone to disregard all [dreams] and say they have no purpose. And yet all through the scriptures there were recorded incidents where the Lord, by dreams, has directed His people. . . . We too may have a dream that may direct us as a revelation."[129]

So how do you know if a dream is from God? One criterion is explained by Elder Richard G. Scott: "Inspired communication in the night is generally accompanied by a sacred feeling for the entire experience."[130] Another guiding factor can be found in 2 Timothy 7:1: "For God hath not given us the spirit of fear; but of power, and of love, and of a sound mind." In other words, a dream that leaves you feeling afraid, confused, or disturbed isn't from God. Nor is one that contradicts the revelations received by the prophets. On the other hand, if the dream "leadeth [you] to do good—yea, to do justly, to walk humbly, to judge righteously . . . this is [God's] Spirit" (D&C 11:12), for "all things which are good cometh of God" (Moroni 7:12). The more adept you are at recognizing the Holy Ghost during your waking hours, the more you'll be able to recognize His influence in your dreams as well.

Another way to know if a dream is from God is simply to ask Him in prayer. In response, you may feel a "stupor of thought" (D&C 9:9), indicating it was just an inconsequential dream. Or you may feel the Spirit begin to reveal the meaning and importance of the dream as you commune with God to understand its interpretation. This is what Nephi did with his father's vision of the tree

---

128. "Sometimes I think that my dreams might have real importance. How can I tell whether they have a meaning or are just random?" *New Era*, Oct. 2014, 40.
129. Harold B. Lee, "Revelation and You," *Ensign*, Feb. 1980.
130. Richard G. Scott, "How to Obtain Revelation and Inspiration for Your Personal Life," *Ensign* or *Liahona*, May 2012, 46.

of life, afterward testifying to his brothers that "if ye will . . . ask [God] in faith, believing that ye shall receive, with diligence in keeping [His] commandments, surely these things shall be made known unto you" (1 Nephi 15:11). In this same way, you can know *when* you've had a revelatory dream and *what* God wanted to teach you through it. It's especially helpful to record such experiences immediately upon awaking, since dreams have a tendency to quickly fade away.

If the Lord sees fit to bless you with "visions of the night" (Genesis 46:2), be sure to treat them with reverence, just like with all revelations the Spirit gives you. And, of course, strive to respond according to the guidance you receive. By doing so, you show Heavenly Father that He can trust you with such sacred revelations. As President Harold B. Lee said, "Oh, how grateful we ought to be if the Lord sends us a dream in which is revealed to us the beauties of the eternity or a warning and direction for our special comfort."[131]

Liken to Yourself

- Do you recall ever receiving revelation in the form of a dream? If so, what was the experience like, and what did you learn from it?
- What's one thing you can change in your life to become more worthy of receiving revelation, including through dreams? What could you do before bed to create a more spiritual atmosphere, thus increasing the chances that the Spirit will communicate with you by way of a dream?

131. Harold B. Lee, "Revelation and You," *Ensign*, Feb. 1980.

W

Warns You of Danger

"It is vital to our physical and spiritual safety that we keep the gift of the Holy Ghost."
(Elder Gary E. Stevenson)[132]

This Will Help When . . .

- You want to keep yourself physically safe.
- You want to keep yourself spiritually safe.

Overview

President James E. Faust once said, "Not having the gift of the Holy Ghost is somewhat like having a body without an immune system."[133] One health institute explained that your immune system "protects your body from harmful substances," and "if it stops working properly . . . you get ill."[134] Likewise, the Holy Ghost can offer you great protection—from both physical and spiritual harm—if you keep His influence strong in your life and heed His warnings.

---

132. Gary E. Stevenson, "How Does the Holy Ghost Help You?," *Ensign* or *Liahona*, May 2017, 120.
133. James E. Faust, "Born Again," *Ensign*, May 2001, 58.
134. National Center for Biotechnology Information, "How does the immune system work?," ncbi.nlm.nih.gov.

In terms of physical protection, examples abound. Anciently, Nephi was warned to separate himself from his brothers, thus protecting his family from destruction (see 2 Nephi 5:5). Joseph, Mary's husband, was warned to take his family to Egypt in order to protect Jesus from the wicked King Herod (see Matthew 2:13). As for modern examples, one young father "was awakened one night by a voice that clearly told him to get up and go downstairs," and when he did, he found his kitchen engulfed in flames and was able to save his family from the fire.[135] A mission president in Japan was prompted to invite all his missionaries to a certain meeting, which ended up protecting them from a 9.0-magnitude earthquake and tsunami.[136] Such physical protection is available to you too as you heed the promptings of the Spirit.

As for spiritual protection, the Holy Ghost can warn you of things that would be detrimental to your spiritual development. For example, He may caution you against starting to watch a certain TV show that would end up wasting your time and/or filling your mind with material contrary to God's commandments. He might counsel you to distance yourself from someone whose influence is leading you away from God. Or, before clicking on what appears to be a harmless link online, He may prompt you to not click on it, thus protecting you from immoral content you didn't know was there.

The Spirit is particularly adept at guarding you against temptations—helping you avoid and resist them—especially when it comes to your weaknesses. As Doctrine and Covenants 62:1 teaches, "Jesus Christ, your advocate . . . knoweth the weakness of man and how to succor them who are tempted." One way He will succor you is through the guiding and protective influence of the Holy Ghost.

It's important to note that warnings from the Spirit don't always have to be regarding dire, life-or-death situations. He can

---

135. *Duties and Blessings of the Priesthood: Basic Manual for Priesthood Holders, Part A* (2000), 226–227.

136. Gary E. Stevenson, "How Does the Holy Ghost Help You?," 119.

do something as simple as telling you to "check the pockets" when putting jeans in the washer, thus preventing you from washing—and therefore ruining—an expensive pair of headphones. Or he might cause you to pause just before saying something to someone that would do more harm than good. Consider the Holy Ghost as a friend who is constantly looking out for you—in both big and small ways.

It can feel strange to heed warnings that don't always seem to make sense, but that's how the Spirit often works—giving us a firm "what to do" without a clear "why to do it." Sometimes you'll see the beneficial results of following these warnings, but other times you won't. However, by continually heeding the voice of the Spirit, you will learn firsthand that "the Lord preserveth all them that love him" (Psalm 145:20). You can also take comfort in the powerful promise by President Boyd K. Packer that "no member of this Church . . . will ever make a serious mistake without first being warned by the promptings of the Holy Ghost."[137]

Liken to Yourself

- When do you recall heeding a warning from the Spirit? How have you been blessed by heeding such promptings?
- Do you ever recall ignoring a warning from the Spirit? If so, why did you ignore it, and what were the consequences of doing so?

137. Boyd K. Packer, "How to Survive in Enemy Territory," *New Era*, Apr. 2012, 3.

X

Helps You **Examine** Your Life

"As often as thou hast inquired thou hast received instruction of my Spirit. If it had not been so, thou wouldst not have come to the place where thou art at this time." (D&C 6:14)

This Will Help When . . .

- You'd like to know what God would have you change in your life.
- You want to make changes in your life but you're not sure where to start.

Overview

Matthew 5:48 contains what is perhaps the most difficult charge in all the scriptures: "Be ye therefore perfect, even as your Father which is in heaven is perfect." Church leaders have clarified that this process of perfection is eternal,[138] but still, God expects you to make as much progress as possible in this life. Thankfully you don't have to do this alone. The Holy Ghost can help you examine your life and make incremental changes that will move

---

138. Jeffrey R. Holland, "Be Ye Therefore Perfect—Eventually," *Ensign* or *Liahona*, Nov. 2017.

you forward on the path to perfection. As the popular saying goes, "There's only one way to eat an elephant—one bite at a time," and the Spirit can help you know just what "bite" to take right now.

The best way to know how you can progress is to inquire of the Lord and then pay attention to the impressions that come through the Holy Ghost. For example, Sister Michelle D. Craig shared that she often asks herself two questions: "What am I doing that I should stop doing?" and "What am I not doing that I should start doing?"[139] Such simple questions open the channels of communication with the Spirit, who can help you grow "from grace to grace" (D&C 93:13) in small but significant ways.

Other questions you can ask can be found in Elder Larry R. Lawrence's powerful talk "What Lack I Yet?" He shares the experiences of several people who humbly and courageously asked, "What is keeping me from progressing?" "What do I need to change?" and "What can I do to improve my life?" In every case, the Holy Ghost answered with "customized counsel" that was clear, simple, and very effective in helping them become better and happier. What a blessing it is to have "a completely honest companion [who] will tell us things that no one else knows or has the courage to say."[140]

You might be hesitant to ask such questions because you're afraid of being bombarded with answers. But the Spirit doesn't work that way. Elder Lawrence explained:

> The Holy Ghost doesn't tell us to improve everything at once. If He did, we would become discouraged and give up. The Spirit works with us at our own speed, one step at a time, or as the Lord has taught, "line upon line, precept upon precept, . . . and blessed are those who hearken unto my

139. Michelle D. Craig, "Eyes to See," *Ensign* or *Liahona*, Nov. 2020, 16.
140. Larry R. Lawrence, "What Lack I Yet?," *Ensign* or *Liahona*, Nov. 2015, 34.

precepts, . . . for unto him that receiveth I will give more" [2 Nephi 28:30].[141]

It can still be difficult to receive correction and direction from the Spirit, but the more you do it, the more you'll realize how much your Heavenly Father loves you. As Elder Jeffrey R. Holland taught, "God doesn't care nearly as much about where you have been as He does about where you are and, with His help, where you are willing to go."[142] Just as "God sent not his Son into the world to condemn the world; but that the world through him might be saved" (John 3:17), He also doesn't send His *Spirit* to condemn you, but rather to lovingly guide you away from sin and toward the blessings of righteousness.

Lastly, as you "consider your ways" (Haggai 1:5), don't forget to pause occasionally and look back at how far you've come. President Henry B. Eyring counseled, "As you examine your life . . . I hope your thoughts center not only on things you have done wrong but also on things you have done right. . . . When I have done this, the Spirit has reassured me that while I'm still far from perfect, I'm better today than I was yesterday. And this gives me confidence that, because of the Savior, I can be even better tomorrow."[143]

By heeding the Spirit's promptings about how to further progress in your life, you will experience the Lord's promise that "he that receiveth light, and continueth in God, receiveth more light; and that light groweth brighter and brighter until the perfect day" (D&C 50:24). That perfect day is when *you* will truly be "perfect, even as your Father which is in heaven is perfect" (Matthew 5:48).

141. Ibid., 34.
142. Jeffrey R. Holland, "'Remember Lot's Wife': Faith Is for the Future" (Brigham Young University devotional, Jan. 13, 2009), speeches.byu.edu.
143. Henry B. Eyring, "Always Remember Him," *Ensign*, Feb. 2018, 5.

Liken to Yourself

- When you ask yourself and God the following two questions, what does the Spirit bring to mind? "What am I doing that I should stop doing?" "What am I not doing that I should start doing?" How do you feel about this counsel, and what can you do to follow it?
- When you reflect on "things you have done right" and ways in which you've grown spiritually, what comes to mind? Why do you think it's important to remember past progress instead of just focusing on what still needs to be done?

Y

Reveals ***Your*** Life Mission

"Before I formed thee in the belly I knew thee; and before thou camest forth out of the womb I sanctified thee, and I ordained thee." (Jeremiah 1:5)

This Will Help When . . .

- You want to better understand your purpose in life.
- You need help determining how to best spend your time and what endeavors to pursue.

Overview

Many Church members are familiar with the doctrine of foreordination. As explained by Elder Bruce R. McConkie, "The Lord foreordained chosen spirit children in pre-existence and assigned them to come to earth at particular times and places so that they might aid in furthering his divine will. These pre-existence appointments . . . designated certain individuals to perform missions which the Lord in his wisdom knew they had the talent and capacities to do."[144] It's easy to read this and think it's talking about prophets and other prominent leaders, but did you know that foreordination

144. Bruce R. McConkie, *Mormon Doctrine*, 2nd ed. (1966), 290.

pertains to *you* as well? In fact, "the doctrine of foreordination applies to *all* members of the Church, not just to the Savior and His prophets."[145]

So, what then were you foreordained to do? In other words, what is *your* life mission? That is something the Holy Ghost can reveal to you over time.

Similar to the advice in the previous chapter, a little inquiring of the Lord can go a long way in helping you answer these questions. Randal A. Wright, author of *Achieving Your Life Mission*, put it this way: "If [Heavenly Father] sent you to earth with a specific mission to perform, don't you think he would be eager to tell you what it was? You need to 'ask in faith, nothing wavering' [James 1:6]."[146] He goes on to offer the following advice: "I challenge you to write down the following question: *What mission was I sent to earth to perform?* Then over the course of days, weeks, months, and even years record the promptings that come to you when you ponder the question and listen for answers."[147] The Spirit will surely answer your sincere pleas as you seek to know God's will for you and your life.

Another way the Holy Ghost will guide you is by encouraging you in those endeavors that most align with your life mission. Some decisions will just feel "right" to you, which is the Spirit's way of telling you to move forward. On the other hand, some will feel "wrong"—even pursuits that have nothing inherently wrong with them—which is the Spirit's way of nudging you away from that which would ultimately not be best for you. Likewise, pay attention to the things you're good at, the things that invigorate you, and the things you enjoy—even when they're difficult. Some of the fruits of the Spirit are "love, joy, peace, [and] longsuffering" (Galatians 5:22), so anytime you have such feelings, you can be confident you're on the right track.

The task of figuring out your life mission—not to mention the task of *fulfilling* that mission—can seem daunting. But don't fall into the trap of thinking that a life mission entails just one thing, like pursuing

---

145. Gospel Topics, "Foreordination," topics.ChurchofJesusChrist.org; emphasis added.
146. Randal A. Wright, *Achieving Your Life Mission* (2009), 23.
147. Ibid., 28.

a single career or using just one particular talent to bless others. Yes, some may find that the Spirit strongly urges them to pursue a certain path. But for others, the Holy Ghost may give much more leeway, approving a variety of options. For example, a life mission of "helping people realize and achieve their potential" can be equally achieved by a caring therapist, an insightful blog writer, or simply a man or woman who constantly seeks to lift those around them.

Lastly, the details of your life mission may change over time as your circumstances change. As Ecclesiastes teaches us, "To every thing there is a season, and a time to every purpose under the heaven" (Ecclesiastes 3:1). As long as you keep the Holy Ghost as your companion, He can help you navigate any season, revealing to you what God would have you do with your time and talents at that particular time in your life.

The poet James Russell Lowell once said, "No man is ever born into the world whose work is not born with him. Everyone has a job to be done which he is supposed to do and which he can do better than anyone else in the world."[148] Make no mistake about it—*you* have a work to do in this life. And "if thou shalt ask, thou shalt receive revelation upon revelation" (D&C 42:61) from the Holy Ghost, making that mission known to you.

Liken to Yourself

- Follow the suggestion to write down the question, *What mission was I sent to earth to perform?* What promptings do you receive from the Spirit in response to this?
- What are some things you enjoy doing and/or seem to have a natural talent for? How could you use these things to help God and His children?
- If you've received your patriarchal blessing, what insights do you gain from it regarding your life mission? What's one thing you can do to better fulfill the counsel given in your patriarchal blessing?

---

148. Randal A. Wright, *Achieving Your Life Mission* (2009), 8.

Z

Increases Your **Zeal** for the Gospel

"The Spirit of the Lord Omnipotent . . . has wrought a mighty change in us, or in our hearts, that we have no more disposition to do evil, but to do good continually." (Mosiah 5:2)

This Will Help When . . .

- You're in a spiritual rut and want to get out.
- You want to increase your enthusiasm for gospel study and gospel living.
- You'd like your desires to be more righteous.

Overview

The definition of *zeal* is "fervor for a person, cause, or object; eager desire or endeavor; [or] enthusiastic diligence."[149] You can find plenty of examples of righteous zeal in the scriptures, such as the description of the Anti-Nephi-Lehies in Alma 27:27: "They were also distinguished for their zeal towards God, and also towards men." The sons of Mosiah displayed zeal in their desire to preach to the Lamanites, being "desirous that salvation should be declared to every creature" (Mosiah 28:3), and King Lamoni demonstrated his

149. "Zeal," Dictionary.com.

zeal when he humbly told Heavenly Father, "I will give away all my sins to know thee" (Alma 22:18).

But the problem is that we don't always feel this way, do we? Maybe you sometimes keep the commandments as if on autopilot, not thinking about what you're doing or why you're doing it. Or you simply become "weary in well doing" (Galatians 6:9) and just want to take a break. Or, quite possibly, there are parts of gospel living that you just have a hard time doing. Instead of experiencing "enthusiastic diligence," you may find yourself feeling spiritually "lukewarm" (Revelation 3:16) and filled with apathy, fatigue, or reluctance.

So what can be done in situations like this? Is there a way to escape such negative feelings and replace them with zeal instead? Yes! And, as you may have guessed by now, the answer lies in the Holy Ghost.

Philippians 2:13 teaches that "it is God which worketh in you both *to will* and *to do* of his good pleasure." Note the two phrases here: "to will" (desire) and "to do" (act). In other words, the Spirit of God won't just help you *do* what's right—He'll actually help you *want* to do what's right. And, as Elder Neal A. Maxwell taught, "Even a spark of desire can begin change."[150]

This principle certainly isn't new. In fact, here's just a sampling of counsel from Church leaders about developing righteous desires:

- "Pray for the desire to do what is right."[151]
- "Pray for desire to help with this vital part of the work of salvation (missionary work)."[152]
- "Pray for a desire to forgive."[153]

---

150. Neal A. Maxwell, "'According to the Desire of [Our] Hearts'," *Ensign*, Nov. 1996.
151. David E. Sorensen, "You Can't Pet a Rattlesnake," *Ensign*, May 2001, 42.
152. Dallin H. Oaks, "Sharing the Restored Gospel," *Ensign* or *Liahona*, Nov. 2016, 58.
153. *New Testament Study Guide for Home-Study Seminary Students* (manual, 2016), 50.

- "Pray for the desire to love, honor, and follow those who hold the apostleship."[154]

All of these things—choosing the right, preaching the gospel, forgiving others, and accepting prophetic teachings—aren't always easy to do. And that's exactly why praying for *desire* is the right place to start. Because "even if ye can no more than desire to believe, [you can] let this desire work in you" (Alma 32:27) until you're able to move forward in faith. Praying for a righteous desire—and then exercising enough faith to act on that desire—will bring an increased measure of the Holy Ghost and "add to [your] spiritual momentum."[155] As a result, you will feel your zeal for the gospel increase.

You may be surprised to learn that even prophets have found themselves in spiritual ruts, having lost their zeal for a time. At least this was the case for Jeremiah. After being smitten and put in the stocks, there was a moment when he just wanted to give up: "I am in derision daily," he complained, and "every one mocketh me" (Jeremiah 20:7). Then he said to himself, "I will not make mention of [the Lord], nor speak any more in his name" (v.9). In other words, "I've had enough. I can't do this anymore. I'm done."

Now, if that were the end of the story, we'd likely only have twenty chapters in the book of Jeremiah instead of the full fifty-two. But thankfully, such feelings of despair didn't last. Jeremiah ended his account with this description: "But his word was in mine heart as a burning fire shut up in my bones, and I was weary with forbearing, and I could not stay" (Jeremiah 20:9).

This is the effect the Holy Ghost can have on you. He can kindle a spiritual fire within you, so much so that you will "have no more disposition to do evil, but to do good continually" (Mosiah 5:2). He can fill you with righteous desires and elevate your enthusiasm

---

154. Andrew C. Skinner, "Apostasy, Restoration, and Lessons in Faith," *Ensign*, Dec. 1995.
155. Neal A. Maxwell, "'According to the Desire of [Our] Hearts'."

for the gospel. And He can increase your fervor for building the kingdom of God.

So, when you find yourself in a spiritual rut, lacking zeal, don't just stay there. Reach out to God and ask Him to purify and "educate [your] desires" through the power of the Holy Ghost. After all, "everything depends—initially and finally—on our desires. [They] shape our thought patterns . . . precede our deeds, and lie at the very cores of our souls, tilting us toward or away from God."[156] May we all seek the constant companionship of the Holy Ghost, who will forever tilt us toward God.

Liken to Yourself

- How have you noticed your desires become more righteous throughout your life? How have these righteous desires blessed you and others?
- What are some examples of unrighteous desires that you may harbor? What effect do these have on your life?
- How much zeal for the gospel would you say you feel right now? What can you do to increase it?

---

156. Neal A. Maxwell, "'Swallowed Up in the Will of the Father'," *Ensign*, Nov. 1995.

Conclusion

Now that you know the many ways the Spirit can bless you, you may be wondering, "How can I experience all of these blessings?"

The first step, if you haven't done so already, is to receive the gift of the Holy Ghost by being baptized and confirmed into The Church of Jesus Christ of Latter-day Saints. If you haven't received this ordinance, you can most certainly experience the blessings mentioned in this book through the *influence* of the Holy Ghost. However, such feelings will not persist without His constant *companionship*. In other words, "A person may be temporarily guided by the Holy Ghost without receiving the gift of the Holy Ghost . . . [but] this guidance will not be continuous unless the person is baptized and receives the laying on of hands for the gift of the Holy Ghost"[157] by one holding priesthood authority.

If you *have* received the gift of the Holy Ghost, the next step is to truly *receive* Him—into your mind, your heart, and your life—by living worthy of His companionship. You can achieve this by (1) doing things that invite Him into your life, and (2) *not* doing things that drive Him away. On this subject, Elder David A. Bednar shared the following:

> We invite the Holy Ghost into our lives through meaningful personal and family prayer, feasting upon the words of Christ, diligent and exacting obedience, faithfulness and honoring of covenants, and through virtue, humility, and service. And we steadfastly should avoid things that are immodest, coarse, crude, sinful, or evil that cause us to withdraw ourselves from the Holy Ghost.[158]

Additionally, don't underestimate the exceptional power of the sacrament. As you continually witness to God that you "are willing

---

157. *Gospel Principles* (2009), 122.
158. David A. Bednar, "That We May Always Have His Spirit to Be with Us," *Ensign* or *Liahona*, May 2006, 31.

to take upon [you] the name of [Jesus Christ], and always remember him and keep his commandments," you receive the promise that you can "always have his Spirit to be with [you]" (Moroni 4:3).

The more you pay attention, the more you'll notice the presence or absence of the Spirit in your life. This is especially true if you take the time to write down your spiritual experiences in a revelation journal. Elder Richard G. Scott counseled, "Write down in a secure place the important things you learn from the Spirit. You will find that as you write down precious impressions, often more will come. . . . Always, day or night, wherever you are, whatever you are doing, seek to recognize and respond to the direction of the Spirit. . . . This practice will reinforce your capacity to learn by the Spirit."[159]

To follow this counsel, I suggest that you obtain a notebook that you can easily access throughout the day, such as a small physical notebook or a note-taking app on your phone. Then, throughout each day, pay attention to the thoughts and feelings the Holy Ghost gives you, such as moments of peace and comfort, ideas of things you should start or stop doing, insights about gospel principles, or any other blessings covered in this book. Finally, as soon as you have a few spare minutes, record your experience in your revelation journal. Treasuring God's communication with you through the Spirit shows Him that He can trust you. And this will surely lead to additional revelation because, as the Lord taught in the Book of Mormon, "unto him that receiveth I will give more" (2 Nephi 28:30).

Now, another question you might ask after reading this book is, "Can I expect to experience all these blessings from the Spirit all the time?"

On the one hand, Elder David A. Bednar taught that "the Holy Ghost can tarry with us much, if not most, of the time—and certainly the Spirit can be with us more than it is not with us."[160] However, it's important to not expect constant miraculous spiritual

---

159. Richard G. Scott, "To Acquire Knowledge and the Strength to Use It Wisely" (Brigham Young University devotional, Jan. 23, 2001), speeches.byu.edu.

160. David A. Bednar, "That We May Always Have His Spirit to Be with Us," *Ensign* or *Liahona*, May 2006, 30.

experiences. Professor Robert L. Millet wrote that just as "the wind bloweth where it listeth" (John 3:8), so too "the power of the Holy Ghost may come and go, in terms of its intensity and its evident involvement in our lives."[161] Brother Milton Camargo explained it this way:

> I would say that I too would like to constantly feel those strong impressions from the Spirit . . . but I don't. However, what we might feel more often is the still, small voice of the Lord whispering to our mind and heart: "I am here. I love you. Go on; do your best. I will support you." . . . The Holy Ghost is real, and His impressions are real—the big ones and the small ones.[162]

Even though your relationship with the Holy Ghost may vary in terms of intensity from day to day, His companionship can still have a profound impact on your life. And at one time or another, all the blessings covered in this book—from A to Z—can be yours as you diligently strive to live worthy of that companionship.

In parting, I want to wish you the best in your spiritual journey to "receive the Holy Ghost." President Boyd K. Packer once said that "discovering how the Holy Ghost operates in your life is the quest of a lifetime"[163]—and oh, what a quest worth pursuing! I sincerely hope that this book has helped you in this journey, for "there is . . . nothing more crucial to a dynamic Christian life than to spend that life under the guidance and sanctifying power of the Spirit."[164] May God bless you in every aspect of your life as you faithfully seek His Spirit.

---

161. Robert L. Millet, *The Holy Spirit: His Identity, Mission, and Ministry* (2019), 286.
162. Milton Camargo, "Ask, Seek, and Knock," *Ensign* or *Liahona*, Nov. 2020, 107.
163. Boyd K. Packer, "How to Survive in Enemy Territory," *New Era*, Apr. 2012, 3.
164. Robert L. Millet, *The Holy Spirit: His Identity, Mission, and Ministry* (2019), 122.

About the Author

Liz Kazandzhy (kah-zahn-JEE) has worked as a professional book reviewer and top-rated freelance editor, specializing in nonfiction genres such as self-help and religion. But as much as she loves reviewing and editing books, her real passion is writing them. She also enjoys hosting the podcast *Latter-day Saint Book Nook*, where she pulls gospel insights from books of all genres.

Liz served in the Ukraine Kyiv mission, after which she graduated from BYU with a degree in human development. She and her husband, Vlad, currently live in Utah with their three daughters.

Scan to visit

https://lizkazandzhy.com/